Preventing Sibling Rivalry

Six Strategies to Build A Jealousy-Free Home

Sybil Hart, Ph.D.

THE FREE PRESS

NEW YORK LONDON TORONTO SYDNEY SINGAPORE

Although I have taken care to preserve the meaning and significance of the stories of the mothers, fathers, and children in this book, many names and identifying characteristics of individuals have been changed and, in some cases, individuals represented are composites.

THE FREE PRESS
A Division of Simon & Schuster, Inc.
1230 Avenue of the Americas
New York, NY 10020

Designed by Charles B. Hames
Manufactured in the United States of America

1   3   5   7   9   10   8   6   4   2

Library of Congress Cataloging-in-Publication Data
Hart, Sybil
    Preventing sibling rivalry : six strategies to build
a jealousy-free home / Sybil Hart.
        p.   cm.
    Includes bibliographical references (p. 189) and
index.
    1. Sibling rivalry. 2. Jealousy in children.
3. Child rearing. I. Title.
BF723.S43 H346 2001
649'.143—dc21
                                            00-050362

ISBN 0-684-87178-5

To

Alison, Lyndia, and Natalie

Acknowledgments

To the countless mothers, fathers, teachers, caregivers, coaches, and children whose lives touched mine and enlarged it profoundly, I extend warm thanks. My sincere gratitude goes also to a second set of teachers—the generation of scientists before me whose discoveries opened up the field of research on infancy and early childhood and revolutionized ideas about infants and what it means to be human. In particular, I thank Tiffany Field, who made research on infant jealousy a possibility, Jacob L. Gewirtz for his wisdom and mentorship, and Michael Lewis for his insightful observations and respectful criticism. I also thank my colleagues at the University of Miami School of Medicine, especially Nancy Jones and Alexandra Martinez-Tornek, for their helpful comments on early versions of several chapters. Support through a grant from the National Institute of Mental Health (MH 59098) is greatly appreciated. Heartfelt gratitude goes to my literary agent, Gail Ross, and my editor at the Free Press, Philip Rappaport, for their faith in this project and help in launching it. My children, Alison, Lyndia, and Natalie, were the greatest source of inspiration for this work, and to them I owe my deepest gratitude.

Contents

Contents

Introduction

Jealousy is the single most bitter problem in many families, contributing to the phenomenon we call sibling rivalry. In most cases, when seeking advice on how to foster sibling harmony, a parent can count on hearing all sorts of tips on how to defuse conflict, from "just ignore jealousy, they'll outgrow it," to recommendations that parents should space children many years apart. While some suggestions are of use, most include some notable oversights. First, they address problematic behavior well *after* it has been solidly established and without explaining the root of it. How it got there in the first place is never explored. Second, the advice is not always applicable to *your* child or *your* family situation. Not surprisingly, these recommendations, even the best intentioned, fall short of providing any sort of real understanding or relief.

My goal is to explain sibling rivalry *before* there is a new sibling on the scene. Jealousy is usually seen in triangles that include sisters and brothers, but actually it originates in early parent-infant relationships that do not include siblings. Whether you have one or more than one child in your family, your infant's relationship with your next-born child depends on what is happening right now—with you. Just as a kindergartner's math skills are based on lessons learned as early as the newborn period, lessons on siblinghood start early. An infant who starts thinking like a mathematician long before facing numbers in school is an infant who starts learning how to relate to sisters and brothers long before they join the family.

The concepts presented here sprang from my experience as a family therapist, school psychologist, child care center director, and parent, which later spawned a line of infancy studies conducted in laboratory research at the University of Miami School of Medicine. Asking, What is jealousy? and Where does it come from? I developed a new theory that views this often-misunderstood component of personality as both a significant feature of temperament and as a potentially binding force in family relationships. And most important, I found answers that will help parents of infants and young children.

In Part I, I explore the importance and meaning of exclusiveness in the context where jealousy originates: the mother-father-infant triangle. For each member of this triad, the psychology of exclusiveness is different and complex because it operates on several different levels. Part I examines the keys to the three first steps toward preventing sibling rivalry: an infant's innate predisposition, and the foundation of love developed first with mothers and then later, and differently, with fathers.

Part II shares a new technique that we developed during years of research and home observation for assessing an infant's jealousy temperament. You can use this easy-to-follow test to determine what form jealousy takes in your own infant. If you follow the step-by-step instructions you will catch an essential glimpse of your infant's inner nature. Through your understanding of jealousy and the unique form it takes in your infant, you will be armed with insights that can help you decide whether to have another child and how soon this is advisable. This knowledge will help you prepare your child and yourself for the transition involved in having an additional child join your family. I've designed this "how-to" part of the book so that you can refer to it without reading all of the earlier chapters, but I strongly recommend that you read Chapters 4 and 5 before embarking on the project of measuring your infant's jealousy temperament. In Chapter 6, examples and case studies of individual infants and their families drawn from real-life histories will teach you how to interpret your own child's behavior.

Part III helps you set up your future family's relationships. Guidelines show you how to manage jealousy in the parent-sibling triangle, where it is eventually seen. This section of the book explains the keys to three additional steps toward preventing sibling rivalry. Chapter 7 explains the importance of age spacing and why a narrow age gap between children helps unify siblings and families, and Chapter 8 describes the importance of love and how parents can shape the early unfolding of jealousy by first molding the way in which infants learn how to express and evoke love in times of need. Finally, Chapter 9 shows you, and Chapter 10 gives examples of, steps to take in order to defuse rivalry and, most important, build friendship instead.

Sibling relationships *can* be harmonious, especially between close-in-age siblings. The enchanting friendship and companionship that young siblings provide for each other is within the grasp of most families. Once established, these bonds last a lifetime. In fact, the sibling relationship outlasts every other relationship we have in our entire lives, including the parent-child and husband-wife relationship. It is up to parents to nurture the sibling bond. If we set it up right, we can give our children trusted, loyal, and deeply attached friends, their sisters and brothers. And we can give ourselves the boundless pleasure of parenting a joyful family. All of this requires an early start, which is why I recommend that you read this book when you bring home your *first* child.

PART ONE

The First
Love Triangle

Chapter One

Infants

Four Myths about Infant Jealousy

Jealous (adjective). Fearful or wary of being supplanted; apprehensive of losing affection or position. From Latin *zelus,* zeal. See zeal.

Zeal (noun). Enthusiastic devotion to a cause, an ideal, or a goal and tireless diligence in its furtherance. Synonym: passion.

—*The American Heritage Dictionary*

Nothing good comes from jealousy. Indeed, jealousy and goodness are mutually exclusive traits. To most of us, jealousy is the essence of malice and evil. This most reviled characteristic represents the antithesis of kindness, compassion, and virtue. Jealousy is usually suffered by those whose inner lives have been corrupted by harsh early emotional experiences rendering them vulnerable and insecure, or those who have had the misfortune of being born with unredeemably jaundiced souls. To some, jealousy represents mental illness, neurosis, or perhaps a character defect or immaturity. To others, jealousy is a sign of immorality stemming from inadequate religious conviction. For anyone afflicted with jealousy, love relationships are destined to be anything but wholesome or pleasurable, because inevitably, jealousy's poisonous tentacles

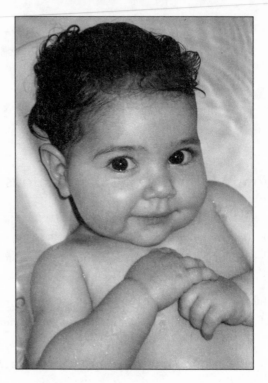

will dissipate love and turn it into hatred. The relationship most tainted by jealousy is that in which it first arises: the sibling relationship.

None of this is true. STRATEGY ONE toward preventing sibling rivalry starts by understanding what jealousy is, and what it isn't.

Myth Number One
Jealousy Starts with the Arrival
of a Second Child

Anna scrutinizes her three-month-old son, Jonathon, fresh from his bath, sweetsmelling and glowing with dreamy-looking calm. She waits patiently for his unfocused eyes to find her adoring gaze. Two seconds, then a third, pass until Jonathon's eyes catch and finally lock onto hers. His face lights up. His eyes and lips widen into a broad expression of surprise, delight, and focused intelligence as if greeting his mother for the first time with, "I recognize you. You're Mommy. Hi, Mommy!" In the blissfulness of this instant, two thoughts cross Anna's mind—wonder at its sheer perfection and doubt about its future. She asks herself, "What would it be like to have another child?"

As parents ponder their firstborn child's adjustment to the arrival of a sibling, they imagine various scenarios. Dad coming from the hospital with the "news." Visiting Mom at the maternity unit. Finally, the big day arrives; baby comes home to stay forever. Sometimes parents foresee their firstborn child reacting like a bomb going off—with an explosion. In other fantasies, the timer goes off more slowly. After a period of adjustment to the newborn, the older child calmly calls a meeting with her parents and in a civilized tone of voice announces that the baby must be returned to the hospital—immediately. Then she explodes. Many of us have imagined the best and the worst outcomes, at one time or another, but one thing for certain is that apprehension over a firstborn's reaction to the arrival of a younger sibling causes parents so much anxiety, even dread, that they actually put off having another child. Most parents assume that the only way to find out how a particular child will respond to a newborn's arrival is to actually walk through the door carrying the newborn baby.

But anguish over how a child will react upon a newborn's arrival is quite unnecessary. The quandary stems from the popular, but erroneous, notion that jealousy is nonexistent until a sibling arrives. If we think carefully about this assumption, we'll see how absurd that is. If it were true that jealousy is nonexistent until the arrival of a sibling, then children who do not have siblings would never become jealous. Yet jealousy is readily apparent in only children and in children from large families alike. Studies on adult jealousy also show that having a phlegmatic or fiercely jealous temperament is unrelated to having siblings. Knowing if an individual is a firstborn or a later-born child, whether he is from a small family or a large family, if he has sisters or brothers, close in age or many years apart, whether he even has siblings, tells you nothing about how jealous he might be.

The arrival of a sibling does not actually *cause* jealousy. Rather, it simply represents the first occasion on which jealousy is typically displayed. In fact, the emotion of jealousy has been firmly formed since the infant's first birthday, usually well before the little rival's appearance on the scene. In my laboratory studies, my colleagues and I induced jealousy by simulating a domestic situation in which mothers simply attended to another child. Twelve-month-old infants were disturbed, and they protested. They did so even if they did *not* have siblings and despite never having seen their mothers behave in this manner toward another child.

Consider a related emotion, anger. Experts know that young infants are capable of experiencing and expressing this emotion. Most parents also know this, often better than we care to admit. But if you are somehow unacquainted with the phenomenon of anger, see what happens to a baby when you offer him his favorite toy and then withdraw it just as he is about to reach for it. Try putting a baby in a swing but do *not* give him a push. Refuse to pick him up so that he cannot see his mother's smiling face as she approaches him after a long day's separation.

These events provoke anger in infants, but only if they have matured to the point where they are intellectually capable of having expectations. Having an expectation requires months of growth during which time infants develop cognitive, or intellectual, skills that gradually enable them to think abstractly. Memory develops so that an infant can think about ideas in his mind, not merely tangible objects in his hands.

Once an infant is able to expect the enjoyment of having an object, such as a toy, he will be enraged by being deprived of it. If he is accustomed to pleasurable experiences, such as being rocked in a swing or observing his mother's approach, he will be angered if they are denied him. Anger ensues from instances where expectations of pleasurable events are violated, or what we call frustration. So infants old enough to have expectations are also old enough to be frustrated and to get angry. Now consider the situation where an infant does *not* express anger and has *not* been frustrated. We don't infer that he is incapable of anger; instead, we can only gather that he has not been frustrated.

Jealousy works in much the same way. Frustrated expectations precipitate jealousy just as they might precipitate anger. In the case of jealousy, however, the expectations associated with jealousy are specifically related to what psychoanalysts have named a "love object," such as a spouse or parent, and how she gives out attention to other individuals. This holds true for adults as well as infants. Infant jealousy is usually a response to a parent's directing attention toward a sibling. Firstborn children are upset by this because they develop the expectation of receiving exclusive parental attention since there are no other children present during the course of the day. Later-born children also develop expectations that spark jealousy. Even though they have not received exclusive parental attention, they have enjoyed the special status of being the youngest child in the family and of receiving preferential treatment, because parents tend to give the youngest child the most attention. Thus, regardless of whether an infant is a firstborn or a later-born child, during early infancy he becomes accustomed to being treated as the "number one" baby. For the "number one" baby, parental attention toward another baby violates her expectations, which leads to a special kind of frustration, known as jealousy.

Anger and jealousy, like all emotions, don't just snap into place. Newborns start off capable only of simple feelings of pleasure and pain, and through increased experience and cognitive maturation, these sensations are elaborated and refined into various distinct emotions. Just as infants do not know how to run without first learning how to sit, stand, and walk, they do not instantaneously "develop" jealousy in the precise moment when a sibling is initially presented. Jealousy emerges through a gradual, though invisible, developmental process in which infants slowly acquire certain kinds of expectations. Through their experiences with parents, infants come to expect parental attention. And they expect it to have certain qualities. Happy babies expect it to be plentiful, prompt, predictable, and tender. Finally, infants expect parental attention to be exclusive, or at least preferential. The process of emotional development that evolves over a period of years is still not fully understood, but it is clear that a simple form of jealousy is established by the first birthday, even though infants have never met their future siblings and have never witnessed their parents attending to another child.

If an infant does *not* express jealousy and has *not* been exposed to a jealousy-inducing event, do not assume that jealousy is nonexistent in that infant. If parents wish to know the status of their infant's jealousy development, they do not need to await the day they confront him with his newborn baby sister or brother. All they have to do is set up a situation that triggers jealousy by violating their infants' expectations of receiving preferential treatment.

Myth Number Two
Sibling Rivalry Is Caused by Changes in Routine and Underpreparation

The arrival of a newborn baby coincides with other changes in family life. Sometimes the changes are so numerous they appear to be overwhelming, especially to a toddler. Baby paraphernalia—old, borrowed, and bought—accumulate from various sources, and are amassed in heaps all over the house. The assemblage might include a bassinet, baby bathtubs, playpens, bottles, cans of formula, boxes and jars of baby food, intercom systems, cameras, video recorders, different kinds of film, photo albums, strollers, walkers, swing sets, cradles and other rocking devices, various infant carriers to strap into a car or a stroller or onto an adult, mountains of disposable diapers, sheets, wipes, pacifiers, nipples, teething rings, baby soaps, lotions, oils and ointments, stuffed animals, toys, games, wall hangings, frescoes, mobiles, audiotapes with songs, videotapes with movies, and clothing that will not fit or be appropriate for years to come.

Preparations for a newborn's arrival will also entail changes for the firstborn child. She may be "promoted" from her crib to a bed. In this process, she witnesses the furniture in her bedroom being rearranged to accommodate the new sleeping arrangements, or she may be moved to an entirely different bedroom. New routines of going to nursery school or child care may have been instituted not long ago. Sometimes families may have just moved to a larger home, in a different neighborhood, where there are unfamiliar children, schools, and teachers. New household helpers and babysitters may also be freshly on the scene. The phone can ring continuously, and unprecedented numbers of neighbors, relatives, and old friends the child has never seen descend on the house.

As the big day gets closer, changes in routine become even more momentous. A mother's departure to the delivery hospital is the most common, now almost universal, change in home life. Even before she disappears physically upon admission to the hospital, her depleted energy resources and preoccupation with the last term of pregnancy may lead to her emotional disappearance, and a young child can feel his mother's moods become erratic and irritable. At some point, the firstborn child is placed in the care of other individuals. Despite a mother's best efforts at finding loving and responsible replacement caregivers, these individuals are unfamiliar with minuscule details of a child's routine, and their care will differ from mother's customary style. A child, no matter how young, even an infant, is keenly aware of changes in his mother's disposition, the presence of new caregivers, and slight departures from normal routine. He feels the air fill with the tension of anticipation.

In view of the magnitude of the changes in household routines, parenting experts strongly and unanimously urge parents to minimize household changes. They recommend that unavoidable changes should be introduced gradually and early in the pregnancy, well before the baby arrives. In turn, parents often go to great lengths to shield their children from changes in routines. Some mothers even choose not to take advantage of hospital facilities, and to instead deliver their babies at home, in order to protect their firstborn children from the stress of separation.

Unfortunately, parents often discover, quite to their dismay, that all of their well-intentioned endeavors failed miserably. Despite their heroic efforts, their firstborn children were jealous when the newborn arrived. Such failure is not surprising given that these efforts are based on the faulty assumption that changes in routine are responsible for jealousy. The prevailing view of sibling rivalry is that it starts with the newborn's arrival and in parallel with changes in household routines. In fact, jealousy has little to do with household routines. In my laboratory research, I discovered that infants were upset when their mothers attended to another child even though absolutely nothing in their young lives had changed. They had *not* been removed from their cribs, put in a new school, separated from their mothers during delivery, placed in the care of different people, or forced to suffer an invasion of relatives and an avalanche of baby paraphernalia, but they were still not pleased by the sight of their mothers extending fond attention toward a rival.

Do your best to keep household changes under control, but don't be misled into thinking that this alone will do the trick. Keep in mind that jealousy is about changes in one's status in a relationship. It is about losing the status of being the only baby or the most important baby in the house. When parents reduce, or even eliminate, commotion around the newborn's arrival, it still remains a fact that the firstborn child's privileged status is being usurped by a newborn baby. The real source of jealousy is as pronounced as ever.

Myth Number Three
Sibling Rivalry Signifies Maladjustment

Psychologists study emotion by dividing it into a number of distinct components and addressing each one independently. For example, we separately consider facial expressions, physical behaviors, physiological responses, intentions, perceived intentions, expectations, consciousness, and self-consciousness. We also distinguish between emotional experience and emotional expression. Emotional experiences may be thought of as feelings, while emotional expressions have to do with actual behaviors. The experience and expression of an emotion can have entirely different meanings. For example, an individual might feel upset, but act calm.

When it comes to jealousy, we judge whether an adult's emotional response is appropriate by evaluating that which can be readily observed, the behavior. We judge actions, not thoughts or feelings, when determining whether a level of jealousy is within reason. No matter how vicious, vindictive, destructive, or perverted one's thoughts may be, if the behavior is under control, we graciously regard the level of jealousy as "normal." The triangular situations that set off jealousy in infants are quite similar to those that provoke jealousy in adults. Indeed, jealousy-eliciting stimuli are fairly constant, even across species. In a variety of animals, including dogs, cats, and birds (as all beloved pet owners already know), jealousy is aroused in comparable kinds of circumstances. But, even though they are similarly triggered and experienced, infant and adult jealousy differ in the way they are manifested. With age, jealousy experiences become increasingly unlinked with matching behaviors, so that a jealous adult can be hostile, but he can also be civil. Adults' emotional feelings and behaviors do not necessarily correspond with each other because adults become adept at masking their emotions, or "acting polite." Infants are not capable of such subtleties. If an infant *feels* jealous, he *acts* jealous.

In infants, as in adults, we judge jealousy on the basis of observable behavior. Unfortunately, we sometimes overlook the fact that in infants, feelings match behaviors fairly precisely. Intense infant jealousy is often taken to suggest that an infant is mean-spirited, selfish, and spoiled by overindulgent parents. Yet, this judgment is unduly harsh. Judging infants by their behavior is probably equivalent to judging adults by their feelings. It could be argued that if adult jealousy were judged on the basis of what adults really think, instead of what they actually do, few people would qualify as "normal."

The notion that a child's intensely jealous behavior suggests maladjustment comes from assumptions based on adult jealousy, which simply do not apply to young children. Toddlers have not been trained, molded, or socialized to act polite when they feel jealous. Moreover, the ability to act polite, or mask an emotion, requires sophisticated mental tactics. A youngster, trying not to show her jealousy, might "put on an act." To do so, she must go through a number of elaborate and intricate mental tasks. She needs to know exactly what constitutes socially acceptable be-havior. She has to use deception, by lying convincingly, to deli-cately trick people into thinking that she really is not jealous. She has to be cognizant of other people's viewpoints so that she can perceive how her own behavior is being interpreted by those who are watching her. All this takes a level of social sophistication unavailable to young children.

Expecting a toddler to mask her feelings is just not an option. In order for an infant to behave less jealous, she has to actually feel less jealous. A two-year-old will not smile at a baby in order to give the appearance of being overjoyed. She will smile at a baby only if she truly feels happy. So, if a two-year-old fails to smile, or if she looks bored when presented for the very first time with the sight of her new baby sister or brother, parents should not be dis-appointed. The child is simply responding to the immediate situa-tion—a wrapped-up bundle, lying in a basket on wheels. A lot of two-year-olds are unimpressed at such a sight.

What does it mean then, when a young child acts very jealous? First, it doesn't represent pathology. Certainly, more research must be done before we can fully understand feelings as complex as jeal-ousy. However, it is already clear that the significance of jealous behavior differs for infants versus adults. In adults, physical aggression and intense hostility are considered pathological. (Even some courts of law will recognize a "crime of passion" as a form of insane behavior.) Evidence suggests that infant jealousy is a normal, healthy sign of emotional development and social bonding. Confirming suggestions based on research with young siblings conducted by Judy Dunn in the United Kingdom, as well as a number of early psychiatric reports, I discovered that the more jealous infants were those who had particularly responsive par-ents. If it were true that infant jealousy signifies maladjustment, then infants of high-functioning parents would be least likely to demonstrate jealousy. But, the truth, in fact, is quite the opposite.

Surely, it seems unfair that more attentive parents are "rewarded" for their devotion by having more rivalrous infants. But this is only one of the paradoxes of jealousy. Perverse at it sounds, intense jealousy may simply mean that the infants have come to have great expectations of their parents because they were nurtured so lovingly during early infancy. This generous interpretation of early sibling rivalry should be heartening to all those dedicated parents whose firstborn children were less than pleased by the arrival of a newborn baby. Although these parents may not recall having enjoyed their firstborns' acting out, at least they can relax with assurances that their toddlers' responses were normal reflections of having been so dearly cared for by their parents.

For parents of infants who seem to show no signs of protest, the news could be less sanguine. When young infants do not obviously appear to be jealous, two possibilities may be entertained. In some instances, the infant may be very mild tempered. Often, a highly sociable child of responsive parents may show only barely perceptible signs of jealousy. Of concern, however, is the less fortunate situation in which an infant shows signs of withdrawal. While it may be a myth that acting out indicates maladjustment, evidence suggests that a flat, distant, quiet, and sad reaction signifies that an infant may be deeply troubled. Later on (in chapters 4 and 5) I will return to this issue in greater detail.

Myth Number Four
Jealousy Is a Fixed Trait

Popular notions hold that jealousy is not present in all individuals. According to this view, jealousy is seen as a sort of trait. Like having the trait for some dreaded disease, we tend to think of jealousy as a characteristic found only in some individuals, those who are flawed. Thinking that there are flawless people out there who

Preventing Sibling Rivalry
Strategy One

Don't be alarmed by the possibility that your infant might be jealous when a newborn sibling joins the family. Jealousy is a normal feature of human nature, and the inevitable outcome of having received our earliest and most tender care within an exclusive relationship.

Instead, use the exercise described in chapters 4 and 5 to learn about *your* infant's jealousy temperament. Knowing the depth of his passion will help you predict and prepare him for a sibling's arrival.

are never jealous is very generous but unrealistic. The news from infancy research is that jealousy is in all of us.

Of course, we are not all alike. Though differences between individuals are not marked by the presence or absence of jealousy, we differ from each other according to our level of sensitivity to exclusiveness, or our jealousy temperament. The many shades of jealousy exist on a broad continuum, all the way from hot to cool. Not only is the jealousy continuum broad, but a lot of extreme behavior will fall within the normal range. When we consider infant jealousy, babies who seem to be well-adjusted and completely typical by every other standard can still show highly extreme behavior. Because the jealousy continuum is completely separate and distinct from other dimensions of temperament, predicting an individual's jealousy response is tricky. Where a particular infant stands on this broad continuum is hard to anticipate on the basis of observing his behavior in most other situations that do not induce jealousy. Difficult, moody infants are not necessarily the most jealous, and easygoing babies are not always the least jealous.

In my studies with infants, I found that even a baby who appears placid and mild tempered can explode in a jealousy-provoking situation, coming as quite a shock to her parents.

Because jealousy appears to be universally present, at some level, in just about everyone, we believe it has a biological basis. But this does not mean that jealousy is unchangeable. Among the widely held misconceptions surrounding ideas of jealousy is the belief that it is a "fixed" trait. Like physical attributes, such as blue eyes or straight hair, many people think of this psychological characteristic as being genetically programmed and invariable. Although blue eyes will always be blue, and straight hair will always be straight, where an infant starts off on the jealousy continuum is not necessarily where he will end up. Fortunately, expressions of psychological traits are amenable to change.

Temperaments are molded through a process called socialization, or learning. For example, a large body of research on shyness has shown that children have an inborn tendency to be timid or bold, but this temperament can be channeled via different kinds of life experiences. When a shy, socially timid child is carefully nurtured by patient parents, his shyness can be overcome. Boosted by parents who cultivate social encounters by providing him with opportunities to learn sports, join teams and clubs, attend parties, and enroll in after-school and summer camp programs, a shy child can become friendly. On the other hand, without such encouragement, the same child may have difficulty making friends or handling new situations. And if he is actively discouraged from being socially drawn out, regardless of whether parents are motivated by well-intentioned overprotectiveness or neglect, the shy child can become seriously handicapped by his timidity. Thus, an innate tendency toward shyness can be developed in either direction, toward greater boldness or greater fearfulness.

Jealousy temperaments can also be channeled. Jealousy can be diminished or it can be intensified. Commonly seen upsurges in acting-out behaviors, aroused by a new baby's arrival, usually subside over a period of time. Warm and playful camaraderie can evolve, sometimes leading to mature and lasting attachments. Yet, in other instances, the problems seem to just get worse. Instead of adjustments, antipathies grow and rivalries become only more divisive over time. In some cases, siblings never manage to bond at all.

What accounts for these opposing trajectories? To answer this, we turn to an examination of the other components of the first triangle, mothers and fathers, whose influences are interwoven with infant characteristics.

Summary

Infant jealousy is not a trait and is not resistant to change. It does not signify flawed character, unsatisfactory bonding, underpreparation, or poor parenting. Nor does it start the day the newborn comes home. Infant jealousy is the inevitable outcome of receiving our earliest and most tender, loving care within an exclusive relationship. All infants come to expect preferential or exclusive care, and all are distressed by the loss of this special status, yet some infants develop hot temperaments, while others are cool. Differences in jealousy depend on an infant's innate predisposition and on the quality of early care. Through a normal and gradual process of emotional growth, experiences with parents shape the way in which early jealousy temperaments are later expressed with siblings. In the following chapters, we examine this process.

Chapter Two

Mothers

The Paradox of Jealousy

He that is not jealous, is not in love.

—St. Augustine, *Confessions*

Raising Emily had been so easy for Pamela. Every tear, whine, or stormy cry could be calmed. No situation was beyond her control; she always seemed to know exactly what to do. Then Adam came along and, from that moment, everything changed. No matter what Pam did in order to bring about peace between the children, nothing worked. The uproar would only escalate, and Pam's spirits only sank. If she tried being firm, she later felt guilty. If she tried backing off, she felt inept. When she wasn't swinging between guilt and ineptness, she felt exasperated and lost.

Why is jealousy so difficult to manage? To answer this question, STRATEGY TWO in preventing sibling rivalry focuses on the arena in which jealousy starts. We look at the emotional core of jealousy and examine how it unfolds within the first love relationship: the mother-infant bond.

Side One

This is how my colleagues and I set up our study on infant jealousy: We created four vignettes, each lasting about one minute and videotaped by a technician hidden behind a partition. In all four scenes, a mother and a stranger (played by myself) sat next to each other while engrossed in a friendly conversation. In the first pair of scenes, we had a recipe book with wonderful pictures of desserts, such as chocolate cake and ice cream sundaes. In the first scene, the stranger held the book on her lap and flipped through the pages, and in the second scene, it was the mother's turn to handle the book. In the next pair of scenes, we fussed over a doll instead of a book. Because of the way in which we held the doll, and because it was fairly lifelike, it looked as though we were holding a real infant. The third episode was enacted by my holding the doll and handling it tenderly, and in the last segment, it was the mother's turn to go through the same motions. Throughout the four scenes, the two of us happily chatted about babies and recipes. In particular, we made positive comments, such as, "Mmm, how sweet!" "Oh! I like this," and "I want one of these!" In the meantime, the infant was on the floor in front of us, being fully ignored.

I hypothesized that if babies are *not* capable of jealousy, then the infants' reactions should be similar across the four situations in which they were being ignored. Thus, Mommy fussing over a *baby doll* would be no more upsetting than Mommy fussing over a *book*. Also, *Mommy* fussing over a doll should be no more upsetting than a *stranger* fussing over a doll. On the other hand, if babies are capable of jealousy, then *Mommy* fussing over a *doll* would be the most distressing situation of all. And that is precisely what was found. As expected, the mother-doll combination aroused the greatest amount of protest in infants.

Behaviors that most parents eventually get to see, but usually not until a newborn sibling arrives, were on full display by the infants who participated in the study, at the time merely twelve months old. Some infants protested a lot, some just a little. And every infant had his own particular style.

The Jealousy Repertory

Miffed by their mothers attending to the baby doll, some infants simply squint their eyes a little, huff once or twice, and then go back to playing. More aggravated ones might also whine and pester their mothers. Slightly distraught infants will tap their feet softly. More distraught ones will smash into the floor or wall with their fists, their feet, or their entire bodies. Assertive infants try scrambling onto their mothers' laps. Less nimble ones will straddle a maternal shin, and then attempt to shimmy their way up to the coveted lap. Sometimes these infants get stuck midway. Suspended by their mothers' skirts, they just hang in the air. Aggressive infants will swipe at the object of maternal attention. Some turn hostile. Eye poking and hair pulling are not unknown, and some infants will even attack their mothers. A bite on the thigh from a jealous one-year-old is not pleasant. Others just go wild with anger. Their faces turn red, their mouths go into a growling square, and their eyebrows dive together over their noses. They hiss, fume, and let out ear-splitting yells. Genuine temper tantrums can occur, complete with kicking, screaming, and thrashing on the floor.

Anxiety takes numerous forms. Thumb sucking, finger twiddling, hair stroking, hand wringing, and nail biting are not uncommon. These repetitive, self-soothing behaviors go together with numerous forms of whimpering and whining. More panicked infants curl up on the floor and rock back and forth. Others rock from side to side while standing up, or they scurry back and forth, up and down the room. Confused babies blink a lot, while looking to the left and right, as if searching for something or someone to help counter their shock and disequilibrium. Others scramble around madly in circles. They can get a numb, unblinking, expressionless look on their faces, and some just freeze up completely.

Fearful infants "stare" at their mothers with their eyes squeezed shut and their shoulders hunched up, or lean back while shielding their faces with their elbows, or disappear by retracting their heads into their shirts, like turtles. Some stand close to their mothers, but with their backs to them, and some hide beneath their mothers' chairs. Others shrink away. Still glowering at their mothers, these babies crawl backward, until they have retreated into the nearest wall. They then slither into the most distant corner of the room, and sit there watching, all crumpled up. In addition to presenting this slumped posture, a sad infant will show classic facial expressions we associate with sadness. The corners of the lips are downturned, and eyelids droop. The eyebrows lift, separate, and raise above the nose, like a drawbridge opening up. Eyes well up with tears. Some infants shed tears and whimper, as they finally start to cry.

Clearly, jealousy protests can be served up in numerous ways, and the repertory is made still more diverse by the fact that an infant's display of jealousy can be composed of more than one emotional reaction in combination, either simultaneously or in quick succession. For example, an infant can scamper nervously back and forth while using one hand to anxiously suck his thumb and his other hand to fearfully shield his face from his mother. Confusion-anger-sadness response sequences in infinite combinations are seen regularly, as infants resort to a succession of different techniques for coping with a jealousy-evoking situation.

Jealousy and Anger

Because jealousy reactions are so individual, the emotional core of jealousy is somewhat of a mystery. One way of getting at an understanding of the essence of jealousy is by asking how it developed in the first place. And so, emotion researchers, like most of us who have wondered about jealousy at some point in our lives, pose the question, Where does jealousy originate? The developmental process responsible for the emergence of emotions has been mapped out with the understanding that some emotions arise early in infancy, while others emerge later. In some cases, emotions such as distress and interest are thought to have no common source and are believed to arise independently of each other. Other emotions are thought to be related to each other sequentially. Precursor emotions are thought to evolve prior to the more complex emotions, just as babbling syllables precedes pronouncing words, which precedes talking in sentences. Obviously, no one learns to speak in sentences before they have a vocabulary, and words cannot be spoken without first knowing the syllables that constitute them.

By a similar logic, emotion researchers believe that complex emotions are derivatives of earlier, simpler emotions. And just as syllables are essential to words, and words are essential to sentences, psychologists feel that simple emotions are so critical to the expression of complex emotions that the existence of complex emotions would be impossible without the prior establishment of simpler emotions. We understand, for example, that surprise cannot exist in the absence of interest, and that shame is impossible without the prior establishment of distress. In search of the emotional core of jealousy, scientists have asked, What previous emotion is at its root? The traditional answer is that jealousy is an outgrowth of anger.

Viewing jealousy as emerging from anger stems from theoretical works written in the 1930s and is still a widely held opinion today. This perspective might seem to make sense, given that anger and jealousy often resemble each other. The problem with this interpretation, however, is that jealousy and anger do not *always* resemble each other. As illustrated by findings of my research with twelve-month-olds, many infants are disturbed by the loss of exclusiveness, but they do *not* show anger. They show other emotions, such as fear and confusion, instead. As it turns out, anger is only one of many ways in which infants express jealousy. It receives a disproportionate amount of attention, perhaps because it is the most conspicuous way of expressing jealousy. Whereas a temper tantrum will rarely go unnoticed, other expressions (for example, dejection or anxiety) are more subtle and easily overlooked. Were it true that anger is a precursor of jealousy, we would expect to find that *every* expression of jealousy includes some amount of anger. But for this we find no evidence.

And so, the common thread, uniting all emotional expressions of jealousy, has to be approached via some other route.

The Other Side of Jealousy

That infants showed distress came as no surprise, since the study was modeled after what I had seen in real life. Participation in the study, however, had a peculiar, and unanticipated, effect on their mothers. Turning to their reactions opened up a new outlook on jealousy.

Mothers generally find sibling rivalry unpleasant, and they react with anguish, frustration, annoyance, impatience, and bewilderment. So it seemed only natural to assume that infants' jealousy protests would generate similar kinds of parental reactions in the lab. With that assumption, members of the research team were unprepared for the emotionally charged behavior that erupted at the conclusion of the study. Infants who only moments earlier had been whining, clinging, and pestering their mothers, were now being swept up in their mothers' arms, plopped onto their mothers' laps, and cosily enveloped in warm maternal embraces. Coinciding with this outpouring of affection, mothers glowingly smiled and coyly admonished their infants with, "You're jealous, sweetheart." Some mothers, while showering kisses on their babies, laughingly rebuked them for being "so bad." Other mothers showed the same demonstrative behavior, but instead giggled, "Mommy's bad," and some even gushed, "Mommy's sorry." Who had behaved badly, we wondered, mommy or baby? Needless to day, all those love-smothered babies lapped up every morsel of affection. Instead of having very upset babies, we now had very happy babies. And so, each little four-part melodrama wound up with a spontaneous happy ending.

Do happy infants have happy mothers, and unhappy infants, unhappy mothers? Not always, at least when it comes to jealousy. We had discovered that even though the infants were happier during the book episodes, their mothers were happier in the doll episodes. To explain this emotional mismatch we followed up with studies to answer the question, How do mothers react to their infants' bad behavior? Does jealousy change a mother's attitude toward her infant?

Two groups of women watched a brief segment of videotape, drawn from one of my previous jealousy studies, in which a one-year-old infant is next to his mother, who is seated on a chair with her back to the camera. First, the infant is standing in front of his mother, wringing his hands and whining. Then he grabs a small quilt and starts to beat it on the floor, forcefully and repeatedly, while yelling. Finally, he throws himself on the floor at his mother's feet and starts furiously pounding on the floor with clenched fists, while kicking his feet, and shrieking, nonstop, as loudly as possible. In short, this was a classic temper tantrum. To find out if women's attitudes toward infants' bad behavior depends on whether they think the behavior is motivated by jealousy, I told each of the two groups of women a different story about the event that precipitated the tantrum. One group was given a jealousy story. They were told that the infant had just witnessed his mother caring for another baby. The other group was given a frustration story. They were told that a toy had just been taken away from the infant because it was time for him to go home. Afterward, the two audiences were asked to report on how they felt about the infant.

Both groups of women felt that the tantrum was an expression of anger, and both rated it at comparably high levels of intensity, suggesting that they were equally impressed by it. Reports on how they thought parents would react to the tantrum, however, depended on whether the behavior had been seen as due to frustration or jealousy. The group that had received the frustration story reported that more firmness and less warmth were warranted. By contrast, the group that had been fed the jealousy story reported that less firmness and greater warmth were in line. So, even though both audiences had viewed the exact same behavior, their attitudes differed. If they believed that the outburst was motivated by jealousy, they showed leniency.

Why is it that frustration and jealousy, though they look the same, get different reactions? Why are women soft on jealousy?

Jealousy and Love

When psychologists analyze emotions, they do so by recognizing various components that make up an emotion, such as feelings, behaviors, facial expressions, and intentions. When theorists have mapped out the process through which emotions develop, they have done so primarily through a focus on emotional behavior, how emotions are expressed through smiles, frowns, and grimaces. But there have been exceptions. A notable one was proposed by Charles Darwin.

Darwin's firstborn son, nicknamed Doddy, was born in 1837. Partly as an adoring parent, and partly as an unsurpassed scientist fascinated by human emotion, Darwin tracked various spontaneous and induced emotional expressions as they emerged in his infant son. One of the induced expressions was jealousy, which was provoked in Doddy by his father holding a doll like a real infant. Darwin kept an account of his son's emotional growth and development, which he published as "A Biographical Sketch of an Infant" in the scientific journal *Mind*, in 1877. The following excerpt includes Darwin's discussion of Doddy's jealousy, anger, and love, which he referred to as "affection":

ANGER—When nearly four months old, and perhaps much earlier, there could be no doubt, from the manner in which the blood gushed into his whole face and scalp, that he easily got into a violent passion. A small cause sufficed; thus, when a little over seven months old, he screamed with rage because a lemon slipped away and he could not seize it with his hands. When eleven months old, if a wrong plaything was given him, he would push it away and beat it . . .

AFFECTION—This probably arose very early in life, if we may judge by his smiling at those who had charge of him when under two months old; though I had no distinct evidence of his distinguishing and recognizing anyone until he was nearly four months old. When nearly five months old, he plainly showed his wish to go to his nurse. But he did not spontaneously exhibit affection by overt acts until a little above a year old, namely, by kissing several times his nurse who had been absent for a short time. With respect to the allied feeling of sympathy, this was clearly shown at 6 months and 11 days by his melancholy face, with the corners of his mouth well depressed, when his nurse pretended to cry. Jealousy was plainly exhibited when I fondled large doll, and when I weighed his infant sister, he being then 15 months old. Seeing how strong a feeling jealousy is in dogs, it would probably be exhibited by infants at an earlier age than that just specified, if they were tried in a fitting manner.

Like women in our earlier study, who were lenient on an infant whose tantrum was attributed to jealousy, Darwin, himself, was a softy. He characterized Doddy's frustration as "violent passion" and "rage," and elsewhere, he also depicted jealousy as "rage," suggesting that he recognized similarities between manifestations of frustration and jealousy. Notwithstanding the obvious correspondence between these two emotional expressions, in this description of Doddy's emotional development, Darwin attributed infant frustration to the emotion of anger, while jealousy was described as a form of affection. For Darwin, jealousy was included among a number of tender behaviors such as hugs, kisses, and sympathy. Clearly, these fond expressions do not bear a strong physical resemblance to each other, and they certainly do not look anything like jealousy. In fact, it is difficult to imagine two acts more unmistakably dissimilar in appearance than an act of jealousy and a deeply sought embrace. For Darwin, congruity between these disparate emotional behaviors rested on something other than appearance.

Each one, in its unique way, signifies the presence of love. Infants do not seek hugs from strangers; they do not kiss people for whom they have no feelings; and they do not get jealous when an unfamiliar adult attends to another baby. Jealousy, like hugs and kisses, is given out selectively. It is reserved for individuals to whom infants are attached. Thus, Doddy, who was portrayed by his father as a jealous baby, was also described, later in the very same article by Darwin, as "truthful, open, and tender, as anyone could desire." It appears that to Darwin, love and jealousy were not incompatible. So, conceptually and in real life—as many of us know firsthand—even in early infancy, affection and jealousy are intertwined by a shared element, love.

Perhaps, in adults as well as in infants, the emotion that runs as a common thread through the myriad of jealousy responses is love. Jealousy, however shown and no matter how unpleasant, is inconceivable without some trace of love. Temperaments are constant features of personality. But in some situations they live inside us, quiet and unseen, and in others they come to the forefront. Just as timidity is a temperament brought out in circumstances marked by novelty, jealousy is a temperament brought out in situations marked by some challenge to an exclusive relationship. And just as timidity cannot be elicited in an infant unless she is somewhat aware that a situation has novel features, jealousy cannot be elicited unless an infant has some sense of his exclusive status in a relationship. The process through which infants develop and prize this special status and the process through which infants develop the capacity to love may be the very same process. Feeling special to someone, and feeling loved, may be equivalent feelings, at least in young infants.

Too bad babies can't talk and, like adults, tell us what they feel when they are jealous. Even an analysis of infants' facial expressions barely yields a glimpse into their feelings. Unfortunately for those of us who study emotion, no single facial expression is associated with love. Our scientific quest into emotion would be so much simpler if there existed some facial gesture specific to love. If only we had something unique in the face to look for, like a special smile, or a particular twist of the eyebrows, that we could uphold as evidence of love, just as we look for smiles to suggest the presence of joy, and frowns to convey displeasure. But love is not easily evidenced by facial expressions, as are joy or displeasure. Thus, we are forced to rely on the presence of certain behaviors, especially in preverbal infants, to signify the presence of love. And one of these behaviors is jealousy protest. Evidence from research suggests that infants are capable of jealousy by the time they reach their first birthday, and, regardless of the form it takes, I would submit that the one-year-old's display of jealousy is evidence of the prior existence of love. In this model, jealousy is conceptualized not on the basis of *how* it is expressed but rather on the basis of *what* it says.

Preventing Sibling Rivalry
Strategy Two

The mother-infant relationship is the bedrock on which infants develop expectancies of exclusiveness. Besides spawning a divisive force, jealousy, the expectancy of exclusiveness is responsible for the emergence of a cohesive force, the emotion of love. In turn, an infant's expression of jealousy communicates both love and anguish. These diametrically opposed and powerful messages are inherent in every expression of infant jealousy, and they leave mothers feeling pulled in opposite directions.

Recognize a young child's jealousy as normal, but do not succumb to confusion over its mixed signals. Reckon with jealousy by first disentangling its positive and negative meanings. Then confront each one separately, as shown later, in chapters 8 and 9.

The Arousal Response

Not much is known about the experience of infant jealousy, but scientists have studied how adults experience it. Jeff Bryson at San Diego State University found that adults' primary feeling is "emotional devastation." Adults in his study reported feeling helpless, dazed, insecure, unable to cope, physically ill, inadequate, fearful, confused, anxious, and depressed. The same study reported that jealousy also precipitated reactions characterized by anger. The adults said they felt "anger toward my partner," "angry toward the other person," "betrayed," and "like getting even." More important, besides describing themselves as feeling emotionally devastated and angry, the adults consistently reported that jealousy provocation led to feelings of "arousal." Individuals in the study noted that being jealous would result in their greater desire to pay attention to their partners, to monopolize their partner's time, and to feel more attracted to their partners. Bryson saw these responses as "relationship-intensifying" reactions.

Like adults, infants are disturbed by infidelity. They appear sad, mad, anxious, and confused. And through these emotional displays they, too, are showing what could be described as an arousal response. Regardless of the negative form it takes, whether anger, sadness, or fear are its tone, jealousy protests serve as relationship-intensifying measures. These efforts consist of attempts to win back maternal attention and to reestablish the mother-infant relationship. Indeed, *the* most predictable pattern of response to jealousy inducement is an infant promptly approaching his mother, and then undertaking vigorous attempts to regain and monopolize her attention.

Mixed Messages

How does jealousy go to work on mothers? How do women's soft attitudes actually translate into parenting behavior? Do mothers confront the hatred and anguish, succumb to the tender message behind the furor, or both?

Mothers respond to infant jealousy with a chaotic package of mixed emotions, amounting to double messages, and then some. Their joyous celebrations of an infant's jealousy protests become mixed up with reproof. Infants are told that they are being jealous and bad, and at the very same time, they are being hugged and kissed. Simultaneously, mothers shower their infants with words of love and words of rebuke. An infant who behaves badly can find his mother apologizing for her own behavior, instead of his.

Such contradictory maternal responses, observed in the lab and in real life, mirror the contradictory nature of jealousy. They also foretell the result: irrational parenting.

One of the most telling examples of the upside-down phenomenon that is jealousy was evoked in our study in the few instances where infants did *not* act jealous. Faced with the prospect of an infant's failure to protest, mothers simply fell apart. "Oh no! What if he doesn't care?" panicked one mother at the start of the study. More than one frantic mother had to be coaxed into cooperating by being reassured that her infant undoubtedly *would* protest. (It is not often that a psychologist finds herself providing encouragement to a mother by promising her that if she made some effort she would succeed in eliciting her infant's *bad* behavior.) Nervous mothers were not diverted though, by being reminded that they could simply withdraw from the study. The mothers wanted to take part in the study, just as they wanted their infants to protest. Still, despite their mothers' persistence, a few infants showed no signs of protest. In these instances, instead of having infants who were crushed, we would have mothers who were crushed. Even though their infants were demonstrating objectively better behavior, these mothers were disappointed, and the spontaneous reunion that followed was not a splendid grand finale. No happy endings were in store for these infants. In this instance, good behavior was nothing to celebrate.

To find out more about mothers' reactions to different degrees of infant jealousy, and especially the consequences of dampened levels of protest, another study looked into women's feelings about two toddlers, both viewed on videotape. One group of women was presented with a segment in which a toddler is standing before his mother and sobbing. The second group saw a toddler of the same age, but this child simply approaches his mother and whines and then walks away. The approach-and-whine pattern repeats itself one more time and might be described as mild pestering. Each audience saw a different segment of tape, but both groups were told the exact same jealousy story, that the toddler's mother was attending to another baby. After viewing the tapes, the audiences were asked to speculate about how much they thought the toddler loved his mother. According to the women, the sobbing toddler was the more loving child, while the toddler who only pestered mildly was seen as the less loving child.

Notions that infant jealousy signifies the presence of love, and that *more* jealousy signifies *more* love, is again compatible with what is known about adult jealousy. Studies show that adults' greater jealousy is associated with greater love. Again, it may be the case, in both infants and adults, that we are more susceptible to jealousy as we are more invested in a relationship. Could this have been the thought that crossed the mind of one young mother as she flashed a "thumbs-up" signal and a fierce look of pride as her infant showed a hearty, though rancorous, show of jealousy?

Insightful Parenting

A mother does *not* handle sibling rivalry as if thinking, "In my toddler's jealousy, I hear him telling me that he is mad at me *and* that he adores me. Wouldn't it be a great idea if I responded by telling him that he is being a very good boy *and* a very bad boy." Most mothers have no idea that their infants are sending mixed signals. Even worse, they are unaware that they are sending conflicting signals in return. Mothers' reactions to jealousy are mostly unconscious and unintentional. No wonder they appear irrational.

None of the mothers in the research study had verbally expressed a desire for her infant to demonstrate jealousy. When mothers found themselves overjoyed at succeeding in eliciting their infants' jealousy, they seemed caught off guard. Catching a glimpse of themselves on videotape, some appeared embarrassed by their obvious sense of triumph. As if they had hoped to keep their joy a secret, fearing to share their delight, even with themselves, mothers were ashamed of appearing flattered by their infants' jealousy. To openly admit taking pleasure in it took a level of candidness that was beyond most mothers.

Although mothers may be afraid of what they might see when they look inside themselves, most are well aware of their ineptness; they recognize their ambivalence toward sibling rivalry and their hesitancy to respond to conflicts. Mothers taking weak action against sibling rivalry was observed in a recent study by Lisa Perozynski and Laurie Kramer at New Mexico State University, who reported that the most typical parental response to fighting between children is a failure to do anything at all, leading to a commentary article in *Time* magazine in which parents were aptly referred to as "reluctant referees." To the extent that mothers are at a loss about what to do, hesitant to take charge, and willing to abdicate their responsibilities by simply letting their children sort out disputes for themselves, they are also clueless when it comes to frankly recognizing their own deeper feelings about jealousy. Mothers blur differences between jealousy and frustration and are oblivious to distinctions they make in their treatment of jealousy and anger. Most are blind to the fact that they treat jealousy and frustration differently, responding more leniently toward jealousy. With such cluelessness, mothers don't just feel irrational, they act irrationally.

The challenge in dealing with jealousy is that the sad and angry behavior is disturbing, but the loving message is compelling. At some level, mothers are faced with the contradictory task of trying to squelch anger, but not love. This can be done. The first step is to recognize our mixed feelings about jealousy and to reconcile our positive interpretation of it. For it is impossible to manage our own reactions unless we are aware of them in the first place.

Does this mean that it makes sense for mothers, like those in the laboratory study, to be admonishing their infants verbally, while kissing them? Do mixed feeling have to be matched by mixed behaviors? Certainly not. Those kinds of ambivalent responses to jealousy may be acceptable in a research setting where the only victim is a doll. But in real life, such reactions only result in mothers' unwitting promotion of the very behaviors they ultimately wish to eliminate. Unlike infants, we, as adults, *can* separate our feelings from our behaviors. There should be no shame in taking pride in an infant's primitive demonstration of love. But we do not have to cave in and follow our hearts automatically. We can follow our minds, instead. Doing so, however, starts by at least acknowledging what our hearts tell us.

Summary

Jealousy is not simply an instance of antisocial behavior. And it is not all bad. Rather, it is a two-sided phenomenon. On one side, it consists of negative expressions, which can take a variety of unpleasant forms, as in anger and sadness. But it also acts as an expression of love. If only it was a pretty show of love, like smiles, hugs, kisses, and sympathy, what problems would be solved. Instead, jealousy's intermingled revelation of anguish and love leaves mothers feeling repelled by the behavior, but, at the same time, drawn toward the meaning behind the behavior. Torn between conflicting signals, mothers find themselves inexplicably frustrated, ambivalent, and impotent in the face of their children's jealous behavior.

Having insight into jealousy's double-sidedness is the first step toward managing sibling rivalry. The next step depends on fathers.

Chapter Three

Fathers

Places in the Triangle

Is three a crowd?

—Bill Cosby, *Fatherhood*

STRATEGY THREE in preventing sibling rivalry begins with an examination of the first love triangle, that is, the mother-father-infant triad, and men's status in it. To understand what fathers contribute, we begin by asking, Where do fathers stand? How do they get there?

Men have progressed greatly in facing the important role they play in their infants' lives. Still (to borrow from a well-known slogan), you've come a long way, hubbies, but you're not there yet. The importance of fatherhood is often underplayed partly because tributes to fatherhood are frequently little more than lip service. For example, one well-known parenting expert went to great lengths in mentioning that fathers are completely capable of raising infants. He even went so far as to recommend that fathers should share equally with their wives in the task of child rearing, right from the moment of birth. This is all very well and good, except that elsewhere he sends a very different message. Here is Burton White's often-cited description of a firstborn's reaction to a newborn sibling's arrival:

36

Think of how she must feel. It's as if she were twenty-five years old, married for a year or so, and very happy. Her husband treats her like a princess; she gets every consideration, huge amounts of attention, and plenty of love. Then one day her husband comes to her in a high state of excitement and says, "I have wonderful news for you: next week I'm going to bring someone else home to live with us. She's a full-grown woman a bit younger than you and somewhat better looking; she's going to be our second wife. Now, since she'll be new to the family I'm naturally going to spend more time with her than with you, but I want you to love her as I will. And here's a box of candy to commemorate this happy occasion." This would be a crushing development for any woman. For a three-year-old it is much more than she can handle emotionally. Small wonder that so many closely spaced older siblings turn sour during their third year of life.

This account inspired an enormous outpouring of sympathy for the plight of firstborn children. The main problem with this statement, however, is that it works on the presumption that the mother-infant relationship is exclusive. In doing so, it shows total disregard for fathers, and the father-infant relationship. The fact that infants love their fathers as well as their mothers is dismissed entirely. Such an oversight might have been allowable a few decades ago. But this passage was published as recently as 1995, by which time discounting the father-infant relationship is inexcusable. Excellent studies documenting infants' attachment to their fathers have been around since the 1960s.

A more accurate rendition of the event that White depicted would expose quite a different pattern of betrayal:

Little Princess has two admirers, Mommy and Daddy. Mommy loves and dotes on her, but so does Daddy. Her love for Daddy is

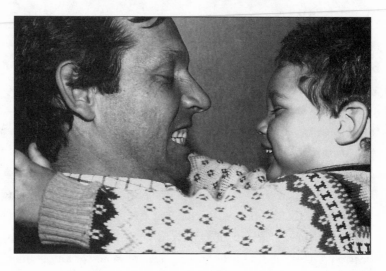

a well-kept secret. Even he doesn't quite realize how much she loves him. One day, Mommy comes home with a new baby. Mommy apologizes profusely and does all she can to make up for destroying what she mistakenly believes is an exclusive relationship. Would Mommy be so sweet and sorry if she only knew that Little Princess had had another sweetie all along?

This more valid depiction of events surrounding the transition to siblinghood should arouse more realistic levels of sympathy for the plight of firstborn children faced with a sibling's arrival. It should also encourage greater sympathy and respect for the underappreciated fathers who love their infants, and whose infants love them in return. Lately, almost every parenting authority, along with mothers, legislators, and religious leaders, is busy hammering away at men, often unsuccessfully, with the message that it is fathers' responsibility to do this and that for their children. Unfortunately, fewer efforts are made to point out to men that while they must share the burden, they can also reap the rewards. Perhaps we have been forgetting the carrot, while doling out the stick.

The Joint Account

The mother-infant relationship is not an exclusive bond. The widespread illusion originates from a number of factors. For one, the maternal perspective differs from that of infants. From a mother's point of view, the relationship really is exclusive. Unless she gave birth to twins, a mother has only one baby, and she is devoted solely to that one baby. Somehow, this kind of devotion leads to a naive assumption, all too common in other types of love relationships as well, that love is reciprocal. So, nearsighted with love, mothers believe that the exclusive love they are extending to their infants is also being returned in much the same way. From an infant's perspective, however, he is in a relationship that is *not* exclusive. It is triadic. While each parent has only one infant, an infant has two parents.

Illusory beliefs in the exclusive nature of the mother-infant relationship stem also from the fact that fathers differ dramatically from mothers in the extent to which they spend time in direct contact with their children. Almost every study on every different subgroup of men, across culture and social class, and regardless of whether mothers are employed outside the home, shows that, compared with mothers, fathers spend less time with their infants. Fathers are on the scene less often, and in some instances they are rarely on the scene at all. So, most of the time, the mother-infant relationship actually has the appearance of exclusiveness. But the *feeling* of exclusiveness and the *appearance* of exclusiveness are not the same thing. For instance, some days, I spend more time with my students than with my children. This doesn't mean that I love my students more than I love my children. Similarly, mothers spending more time with their infants might make it look as though the mother-infant relationship is one-on-one, even though this is not the case on an emotional level.

The appearance of exclusiveness is particularly deceptive because it feeds into a related notion, that infants generate love in proportion to the amount of time they spend with a caregiver. Disparities between mothers' and fathers' allocation of time with their children results in the common belief that infants love their mothers more than they love their fathers. According to this view, love is seen as a sort of commodity, deposited in a little bank account that resides inside an infant's heart, and every caregiver has a separate account. A parent can make a withdrawal, but only from her own account, and only if she has made a deposit. She can only take out as much as she put in.

This "separate accounts" view of love may seem logical, but nothing could be further from the truth. The amount of time an infant spends with an individual and the extent of his love for that individual are not always proportional to each other. Infants form attachments with their fathers much as they do with their mothers, regardless of the amount of time spent with their fathers. Infants need a great deal of tender attention. Few infants became loving and secure children if no one pays attention to them. The fortunate reality is that the amount of time spent in one loving relationship actually spills over into another relationship.

In a sense, infant love gets entered into something more like a "joint account," where any nurturing, loving person can make his "love deposits." The source of love could be a mother, father, grandmother, child care worker, babysitter, nanny, or even a sibling. Everyone makes deposits into one account, and everyone makes withdrawals from that same account. What a parent takes out does not have to correspond exactly with what he put in. As a result, a beneficiary can draw love from an account even though he may have put little into the account. The system is not foolproof, but generally it works well for infants, who can benefit from any source of love. On the other hand, this can be a source of irritation. Sometimes, a more-involved parent (mom, for instance) can resent the fact that a less-involved parent (dad, generally) gets to withdraw more than his "fair share" of love.

In more positive instances, one parent's greater involvement can give an infant the emotional resources necessary for enlisting the love and attention of the other. A father who spends little time at home might wonder how his child could show so much love for someone who has done so little for him. Yet, fueled by love from a different source, a child can, through his *own* efforts, draw an estranged parent into a relationship.

Adults tend to assume that parents influence children and that children, especially infants, are the recipients of attention. But infants and children are not always on the receiving end. Even in infancy, relationships are a two-way street. Parents influence children, and children influence parents.

The Two-Way Street

Infants love fathers as much as they love mothers—which leaves scientists wondering, what's unique about fatherhood?

Some studies found that mothers are more likely to take on caregiving duties, such as feeding, bathing, and dressing, while fathers are more inclined toward engaging in playful behavior. Studies have also reported stylistic differences between mothers and fathers, noting that newborns and young infants are treated more gingerly by their mothers. Twenty years ago, Michael Yogman noticed that whereas mothers are more likely to use placid, verbal forms of stimulation, such as soft cooing, fathers offer livelier, physical play. As infants get a little bit older, fathers become even more physically stimulating and unpredictable. This type of invigorating play is a big hit with children.

Reports of stylistic differences between fathers' and mothers' interactions may also be somewhat exaggerated. More recent studies often fail to show pronounced differences between parents. For example, Tiffany Field at the University of Miami found minimal differences between mothers and stay-at-home fathers. Also, the pattern in which fathers are seen primarily as playmates isn't universal. Many studies find that fathers are no more likely then mothers to spend time playing with their infants. Moreover, mothers spend so much more time with their infants that even though caregiving duties take up the bulk of their time with infants, these mothers still spend greater amounts of time than their husbands actually engaged in play. And so, despite their reputation, fathers, in fact, are rarely their infants' chief playmates.

In general, studies have not found robust differences between mother-infant versus father-infant interactions. As leaders in the field of infancy research such as Michael Lamb, Alan Fogel, and Gavin Bremner acknowledge, subtle differences between mothers and fathers, which turned up in early studies, are not always uncovered in newer studies and seem to reflect chance fluctuations due to culture, current attitudes, and conventional family patterns rather than enduring differences between men and women. Finally, it is still unclear whether the greater boisterousness often associated with fatherhood comes as a feature that is distinctive of men or simply as an incidental feature of maleness, such as larger body size, which coincides often, but not always, with male gender. Tossing around a 30-pound toddler is a workout. Chances are, a 180-pound adult will have an easier time of it than a 98-pound adult, regardless of whether the 180-pounder is male or female. One can only wonder, if men were smaller than women, would they still be so frisky?

Apparently, distinctive features of fatherhood are not easily identified by examining differences between mothers' and fathers' behavior patterns. Instead of asking, *What* do men do with their infants, the quest to identify what is unique to fatherhood may be furthered by asking, *When* do men do what they do, and *Why?*

When and Why

In an infant's eyes, fathers do not place second to mothers. But, in all fairness, it does seem that men assume their places in their children's hearts at somewhat later points in time. At birth, an infant will prefer her mother's voice, but not her father's, over a stranger's voice, although fathers catch up a few weeks later. Trust in fathers develops at a slower pace, so that while infants become attached to both mothers and fathers eventually, the father-infant bond is established subsequent to the mother-infant bond. Whereas the mother-infant bond crystallizes by an infant's first birthday, the father-infant bond may not gel until the second birthday.

There are probably a number of reasons why mothers are first to bond with their infants. Social convention is one popular explanation. In most places, it is customary for mothers to take on a larger role in child rearing during early infancy. A related, and perhaps more fundamental, reason for mothers' earlier bonding has to do with the fact that mothers have a substantial head start when it comes to building the parent-infant relationship. Further, not only do mothers start bonding earlier, they may actually have an easier time. Here is one father's candid, and slightly wistful, take on why:

> As I have so often learned these first years of fatherhood, to parent properly—or, I should say, fulfillingly—men have to rely on their imagination a lot more than women do. From gestation on, a Mom's biological connection to her child—whether she's conceiving it or carrying it or nursing it—is enough to fill her MDMR (Minimum Daily Mommy Requirement), and frequently

waives her from any other expression of maternal joy. Don't get me wrong, she can glow as much as she wants to glow in that first crucial year—she's just not required to. Simply taking care to drink a shake when the fetus feels hungry, or giving the newborn an extra dose of mother's milk antibodies, is a decent day's work. After that she's off the hook. In fact, she can even do it all begrudgingly—weary and cranky and hormonal to beat the band—and still get an E for effort.

Dads, on the other hand, often have to manufacture their own connections in order to reap any parental rewards.

As this writer points out, reaping the rewards of parenthood may be more difficult, and certainly less automatic, for men than for women. Indeed, women have babies, not men. This difference between mothers and fathers does not fluctuate with cultural trends, and it is not merely a frequently occurring coincidence, like mens' larger body size. It is a profound, enduring, instinctual, and unchangeable distinction between men and women. And it underscores sharp contrasts in the process through which parent-infant relationships are formed. For women, biology, via gestation and lactation, drives the early formulation of the mother-infant relationship. It does so with such impetus that a mother rarely needs to rely on her "imagination" in order to "manufacture a connection." The connection is made for her, and fulfillment comes, sometimes even in spite of mothers themselves. Rather than feeling it necessary to intentionally work at creating parenthood, or the pretense of parenthood, mothers often feel as though they have little control over the matter. As her belly expands, as her breasts swell with milk, with every morsel of food she eats, and with every breath of air she breathes, a mother is reminded that her identity as "I" has been replaced by "we." Whether she wants to or not, whether she enjoys it or not, a pregnant or nursing mother is an involved parent, and even a responsive parent.

Biology plays no role in kickstarting the father-infant relationship. Until childbirth, fathers attempting to parent must do so with little impetus but from their own imagination. In general, men are left to rely on a different, and later-to-come-forth, set of cues. Of greatest importance in triggering a sense of fatherhood are gestures emanating from infants themselves.

When an infant is born, fathers are elated. Like women, men are exhilarated, anxious, and excited by the transition to parenthood. With the passage of time, fathers become increasingly involved as they are pulled into parenting at their infants' bidding. The sound, sight, and smell of infants are powerful in their appeal to both mothers and fathers. Cues, such as an infant's smiles, are effective in prompting parental attention because adults, both mothers and fathers, are biologically programed to respond to such signals. Many would argue that on the two-way street between parents and children, parents, not infants, start off on the receiving end.

Fathers may be as receptive as mothers to infants' cues; however, fathers differ sharply from mothers in their dependence on such cues for rousing them into parenthood and summoning them into action, both physically and emotionally. Nothing inside mens' bodies—no morning sickness, no baby kicking, no eruption of milk—constantly screams the message, "Hey, you are a parent!" or "Your baby needs you." Without the benefit of an early, immensely potent, undeniable, innately driven thrust into parenthood, fathers are more reliant than mothers on cues from infants themselves. Moreover, unlike the inevitable influence of biological cues provided through pregnancy and lactation, infant cues come later, and still worse, they are "iffy." Some infants are better communicators than others. And, lord only knows, some men are better than others at fabricating "connections" out of their own sheer "imagination." Consequently, the process of establishing a new identity, as parent, and forming links with children are more precarious for fathers.

Thus, a unique characteristic of fatherhood arises from differences in the way men form bonds with their infants. Because they are less reliant on early and inevitable biological cues, and more reliant on later and more fallible infant cues, bonding poses a greater challenge to men. Whether or not an infant sends signals, and whether or not a father will hear those signals sets the tone for the emerging father-child relationship.

The Turning Point

Fathers' later involvement in parenting slows down the process through which men develop identities, behaviors, and relationships compatible with fatherhood. It also impedes the process through which men are seen by others as being parents. Unfortunately, fathers' slower introduction to parenthood contributes to oversights, such as Burton White's, in recognizing that fathers are attachment figures, much like mothers, in the lives of their toddlers.

This kind of oversight is especially regrettable when it comes to the issue of helping a child adjust to a sibling's arrival. With the aim of protecting firstborns from the harshness of displacement by a newborn, Dr. White's message convinced a generation of parents to opt for wide age spacing between children. His observation, "Small wonder that so many closely spaced older siblings turn sour during their third year of life," seems to imply that the problems of firstborn children could be resolved simply by putting off the next-born child's arrival by a year or two. Not only is the recommendation for wide spacing untenable (and I will explain why in chapter 7), it also overshadows one of *the* most pivotal factors in determining a firstborn's chance of successfully adjusting to siblinghood: her relationship with her father.

Preventing Sibling Rivalry
Strategy Three

If it is up to mothers to create the expectations that generate love, then it is up to fathers to sustain that love when maternal attention is diverted by the more immediate demands of a newborn baby. During this transition period, fathers must be available to pick up where mothers leave off so as to ensure that their toddlers receive tender care continuously.

The newborn's arrival is a turning point in a child's life. It marks an end to her privileged status as the youngest child in the family, and in fortunate cases, it also marks the beginning of a redefined and profound bond with her father.

Having a second child entails changes in a mother's attention toward her firstborn child. Surely, it comes as no surprise that studies consistently report that levels of maternal love and care take a dive during the final stages of pregnancy and the initial phase of caring for a second-born child. This then becomes the juncture at which point fathers are key in setting the tone for their family's future relationships. As Cecily Legg noted, some decades ago, on a child's adjustment to siblinghood, "In this family the secure relationship with father seemed to nullify some of the threat of displacement while mother cared for the new sibling." This clinical observation was later backed up in a study by Laurie Gottlieb and Morton Mendelson at McGill University in which the investigators conducted home visits on two occasions, once before and again after the birth of a second child. Both mothers and fathers turned out to be important to their firstborns' coping with a sibling's arrival. What differed, however, was the timing of each parent's influence. The best adjusted toddlers were children who received maximum levels of *maternal* support *before* their new-born sister or brother arrived, and then maximum levels of *paternal* support *after* the baby arrived. Paternal support following a newborn's arrival helped firstborn children cope and in addition helped establish positive sibling relationships during the early post-partum period. Fathers who were highly nurturant toward their firstborn children had firstborn children who were highly nurtu-rant toward their baby siblings. Thus, paternal empathy and com-passion toward toddlers inspires toddlers' empathy and compassion toward their baby siblings.

Nature works differently with each pregnancy. With the first child, pregnancy thrusts mothers into parenthood and the task of bonding with her firstborn. With a second child, pregnancy actu-ally draws a mother away from her firstborn. And in that interlude, as mothers step back, fathers become essential to the emotional survival of their firstborn children. Without men picking up where their partners leave off, toddlers are left stranded in an emotional void. And so, it is at the point when a second child joins the family that fathers need to be in place, beside mothers, as attachment figures, and as loving, supportive, and involved parents.

Children need their fathers. But, clearly, children are needier at some times than at others. The arrival of a sibling is one of those times when children are at their neediest. Fathers *are* slower than mothers in coming into their own as parents. No problem; it's not a race. As Gottlieb and Mendelson show, firstborns are highly receptive to their fathers' attention at the crucial point when they are stressed by a sibling's arrival and by their mothers fading from their lives. When mothers recede into the background, sometimes they can stay there for extended periods of time. If the delivery was difficult or entailed surgery, if the newborn is colicky, if mothers slip into postpartum blues, fathers are especially needed to step into the foreground, and to be there for as long as they are needed.

Ideally, the father-infant bond is well established by the time a sibling is born. Still, if a father is somewhat delayed in taking on fatherhood, if he is less effervescent than some of the energetic young dads so highly touted in the literature, if a "father" is a co-parent who does not even happen to be male, it is OK. During this period of transition, fathers just need to be there, lovingly, patiently, and consistently dedicated to nurturing their firstborn children, and doing so in a manner suited to each father's own personal style of parenting, regardless of whether his forte lies in rough-and-tumble play, storytelling, or just plain tender affection.

Generally, in thinking about sibling rivalry, too much is made of the discrepancy between the level of attention received by one child over that extended to another, and the fact that a newborn will require disproportionate amounts of maternal attention. In doing so, we tend to overlook another discrepancy: that between what any one child will receive before versus after a newborn's arrival. This before-after discrepancy is responsible for much of what is later seen as sibling rivalry. And whereas little can be done to minimize the extent to which mothers must pull away from their firstborn children in order to stabilize their newborns, much can be done to ensure that a firstborn receives continuous care.

It *is* possible for firstborns to be treated with equivalent levels of attention before and after a newborn's arrival. Mostly, it is up to men to define themselves as primary nurturers. But it is also up to women. They, too, must recognize their husbands as being more then just breadwinners, and must value fathers' spending additional time with firstborn children over enhanced family income. Making a firstborn's emotional requirements a priority is a decision that both parents must share since they both will absorb the financial costs by making do without some unnecessary expenditures. Undoubtedly, families need food, safety, medical care, and shelter. The fancy car and gadgets, however, can wait.

Without fathers stepping in, toddlers can easily become, just as Burton White describes them, "sour three-year-olds." Some studies show that girls are particularly vulnerable to suffer from discontinuity in parental care, and are especially needy of paternal attention. Others show that boys who get into hostile relationships early on with their siblings later show hostile aggression toward their peers. Either way, to their sons and daughters, fathers count. And when a sibling joins the family, they count more than ever.

Awakening

Does jealousy work on fathers much as it does on mothers? Here, in the lingo of psychiatry, is one research team's take on the process through which paternal involvement is awakened: "Indeed, from a family systems perspective, it is reasonable to suggest that the fathers' increased involvement in child care activities following the birth of a second child is, in part, a response to requests for care or interaction from their firstborn children seeking attention from sources other than mothers." Exactly how these two-, three-, and four-year-old firstborns couched their "requests" for paternal care was not elaborated in the study. However, it is fairly obvious that, one way or another, these children were not making polite verbal requests; they were expressing jealousy. This is how it looked in one family:

> Phillip knew that he didn't want to be a parent like his own dad, who had been a distant authority figure to his three sons. But he also couldn't be like his wife, Shelley, which seemed impossible even when he tried. Amanda would squirm to get out of his embrace or worse, scream for Mommy, as if she needed to be rescued from her own father. So Phillip just kept his distance despite

Shelley's nagging him to help out with the baby. The more he withdrew, the more unpopular he became with Amanda, and the more Shelley withdrew in return. By the time Adam came along, three years later, Phillip had almost forgotten how unwanted he had felt and instead found himself almost the exact replica of his father.

A few weeks after Adam was born, Phillip was lying on a blanket with Adam, cuddling and cooing beside him, when Amanda walked in. For a moment, she just stood there looking stunned. Then she flew into a rage like nothing Phillip had ever seen. It took him a second to realize that she was jealous, but when she started swinging at the baby it became clear enough. It also dawned on him that she wanted his attention. In fact, she wanted a hug. So that was how Phillip got to give his daughter an unrejected hug, for the very first time in the three long years since she was born.

Where all of Shelley's nagging had failed, Amanda's jealousy succeeded in conveying to Phillip that he was needed. The relationship between Phillip and Amanda didn't blossom overnight, but it definitely started to progress. Eventually, Phillip learned how to care for a daughter, and prided himself later on for his ability to stuff her little legs into a ballet leotard and comb her hair into a pony tail, barrettes and all, painlessly. By the end of a year, Amanda was, no doubt about it, Daddy's girl.

Darwin was not the only father capable of sparking his infant's jealousy. Whenever studies have asked whether sibling rivalry can be triggered by fathers, the answer has been yes. That firstborns are upset by their fathers paying attention to a newborn, much as they are by their mothers doing so, is hardly surprising given that toddlers are attached to their fathers as they are to their mothers. What is perhaps less clear is whether fathers are sensitive to their infants' jealous "requests" for attention. Darwin was not the only father who sensed, in his child's jealousy, an appeal for love. Many men, like Phillip, are drawn into family life at the urging of their children, not their wives. So it may be that jealousy, so deplored for its divisiveness between siblings, is equally vital in awakening paternal affection. How paradoxical, once again, that a force responsible for challenging one relationship, can, at the same time, give life to yet another, perhaps vulnerable but more essential, relationship.

Thus, gentlemen, I urge you to see what your infant sons and daughters have to say when they discover you with another baby in your arms. Especially if you do not know whether you are loved, or if you have doubts about how much you are needed, follow the steps outlined in the next chapter and let your infants tell you the answer themselves. Go ahead, dip into the "joint account." A sweet little carrot may await you, and it may be there even if your deposits have been less than what they should have been, and even if your place in the mother-father-infant triangle is still undefined, or faltering. Perhaps jealousy will touch a nerve in you, as keenly as it does in your wives, and melt your hearts, just a little.

PART TWO

Your Infant's Jealousy Profile

Chapter Four

How to Measure *Your* Infant's Jealousy Temperament

Ever wonder how your toddler will react to the arrival of a newborn baby? Now there's no need to lose sleep over this question. A glimpse into an infant's future reaction to a sibling can be yours by following the steps outlined in this chapter.

Why Measure Infant Jealousy?

Discovering your baby's jealousy temperament helps you identify signs of healthy emotional development; it can also alert you to the possibility that an infant is experiencing emotional hardship. Your awareness of your infant's emotional status tells you whether your infant is ready to handle a new baby's arrival or is in need of extra time and attention. Chapter 8 provides information that should be especially helpful to families who find themselves confronted by an infant in need of attention.

This chapter describes a two-minute exercise in which you'll be briefly exposing your infant to a situation that he'll eventually face in life, when a real new baby joins the family. Keep in mind that for your infant this scenario will seem real, although the true situation will actually be considerably more provocative. A real baby, who coos and smiles, is certainly more compelling than the lifeless doll used in this exercise. Many parents might wonder if even a few seconds of relatively mild discomfort is warranted. Why let an infant endure even minimal distress? Because the information gleaned through the exercise will be used to the advantage of both infant and the family.

The Exercise

The method for evaluating an infant's jealousy temperament is the at-home version of laboratory research described earlier in Chapter 2. This self-guided exercise is simple, but keep in mind that the most telling insight into an infant's jealousy temperament will be based on observing his *first* reaction to the loss of exclusive attention. And, of course, things happen for the first time only once. So, be ready.

You will need equipment and space, arranged as in the illustration on page 61, and possibly a helper.

Equipment

DOLL. The most essential piece of equipment is the sort of regular baby doll available in most toy stores. Dolls that look like miniature fashion models are not appropriate. Usually, you can find baby dolls in a variety of skin tones and hair colors. Look for one that most resembles your infant. If possible, choose a doll with eyelids that blink and a soft body, since these features help create the impression of a real infant. Some dolls are equipped to make lifelike "baby noises," a helpful addition if the noises are pleasant, cooing sounds, rather than crying. Finally, examine what the doll is wearing. A one-piece outfit, which covers the legs, is usually the best way to disguise the fact that the doll is not a real infant. If your infant is male, consider changing the doll into less feminine clothing, perhaps something from your own child's wardrobe.

PICTURE BOOK. Get a book or magazine that has colorful photographs or illustrations. Many parents use a cook book with close-up shots of tasty desserts, like chocolate cake and ice cream sundaes. The book you select should be new to your infant, so don't use a familiar story book. Also, try to avoid using any book that is particularly valuable because it may get a bit mangled.

CHAIR. An ordinary kitchen chair is all that is necessary. Do not use anything with arm rests or upholstery, as these will block an infant's view of what you are holding in your arms.

CAMCORDER. Having someone videotape is a good option if you wish to document your infant's reactions on film. This allows you to concentrate on conducting your assessment without also having to observe your infant, all at the same time. Videotaping affords possibilities for analyzing an infant's behavior more fully, while also preserving a memento that can be a treasure, of sorts. If a second adult is unavailable, the video camera can be supported on a piece of furniture or a tripod.

TIMER. For determining when sixty seconds is up, use a clock, a wristwatch, a stopwatch, or the timer built into a camcorder.

Space

Choose an uncluttered room that has some open space and no toys. The fewer distractions, the better. If you have someone present to help you, use drapery or a large piece of furniture to obscure their presence.

Helper

An adult assistant can help by videotaping the exercise, or simply by watching it take place. Someone familiar to your infant will be least distracting. Whether by taping or acting as an "unbiased" observer, the assistant's unobtrusive presence helps you focus on the exercise itself.

Preparation

The best age for measuring an infant's jealousy temperament is around the first birthday. This stage of development is late enough for jealousy to have formed, and early enough to provide information key to parents' decisions about age spacing in a timely manner. Deciding whether an age difference of only two years is advisable for a particular child depends on parents being cognizant of her emotional development at one year.

Arrange your equipment in a room that is free of clutter. Remove any objects that are potentially dangerous and make sure all windows and doors are shut tight. Place a chair in a corner of the room, with its back to the corner. Have a clock in sight, and place the doll and book close to the chair, but hidden from view.

If an assistant is going to act as observer, this person should be positioned somewhere behind the chair, and deeper into the corner of the room. Eye contact between the infant and helper should be avoided at all times. This corner is also the best vantage point for a video camera, which can be mounted on a tripod or positioned on a piece of furniture, with the lens focused on the space immediately in front of the chair, approximately where your knees will be. To as great an extent as possible, the observer and/or camera should be obscured from view by drapery or furniture.

Especially in cases where the exercise is *not* going to be video-taped, it is advisable to read ahead, through the following chapter, before conducting the procedure. This will help make you aware of certain features of response that are important clues to interpreting your infant's jealousy temperament. Knowing what to look for will help eliminate a need to repeat the procedure.

What to Do

BOOK EPISODE. Begin the first part of the procedure by entering the room with your infant. Have him bring along a toy that is somewhat entertaining, but not brand new. If he is attached to a particular toy or object, such as a blanket or teddy bear, let him bring that along instead. Close the door, walk to the chair, and sit down. When your infant appears settled, turn on the camera. Then pull out the picture book and put it on your lap. Turn the pages and, using a sweet, sing-song tone of voice, make positive statements about the pictured items, such as, "Oh, I like this. How sweet. I want this one." *Direct your statements at the book and avoid eye contact with your infant.* After approximately one minute, put the book away and then see that your infant is calm.

DOLL EPISODE. Continue with the second part of the procedure by bringing out the doll and putting it on your lap as tenderly as possible. Arrange the doll's head so that it faces your chest, and the back of the doll's head is in clear view of the infant. Rock and stroke the doll affectionately, as if it was a real baby. In a sweet, sing-song tone of voice, make pleasant comments directly to the doll, such as "Oh, I like you. You are so sweet. I want you." Keep this up for about one minute, or until the infant figures out that the doll is not real. *Face the doll directly and avoid eye contact with your infant.* Then put the doll away carefully, so that the infant does not see it again for some time.

If a second adult, usually the other parent, wishes to induce jealousy as well, the exercise can be repeated. Wait a week or so before the next try, and after the assessment has been conducted for a total of two or three times, at most, it should not be repeated.

What If

Stop immediately if an infant becomes too distressed at any point during the exercise. There is no need to continue once a toddler is in distress, since an infant's behavior can be analyzed on the basis of less than the full sixty seconds. Ideally, an assistant is present and responsible for determining the point at which an infant's distress level warrants cutting short the exercise. If an observer is unavailable, however, the individual who is inducing jealousy is responsible for making this judgment while at the same time conducting the procedure. Be aware that some infants heat up slowly, and others react instantaneously.

Repeat the exercise if an infant shows no signs of distress whatsoever in the doll episode, or if he appears more upset during the book episode than during the doll episode. For the repeat try, videotaping the episodes will be especially helpful. The difference between mild jealousy and no jealousy is subtle, but critical. Making a distinction will require analyzing details of your infant's reaction, which can be difficult to do if you are conducting the procedure while analyzing your infant's mild reaction, all at the same time.

Wait a week or so before repeating the procedure so that your infant has time to get used to the room setup. In some cases, infants

fail to respond because they become preoccupied with some odd feature of the setting. If furniture has been rearranged or altered through the addition of cameras, such novelty may have distracted the infant from noticing what a parent was doing. During the time period between assessments, leave the setup in place, including the chair, camera, and any changes in furniture arrangement, so that the infant will not be thrown off by unusual surroundings.

A number of other possible sources of distraction could also have interfered with an infant's response to jealousy inducement. The toy that an infant brings along usually keeps her from becoming too bored in the book episode, but if you feel that it was too distracting, next time use a toy that is less appealing. Also, consider the possibility that the picture book created too much distraction. Use a less colorful book the second time around, but make sure your voice is still as sugary as ever.

Sometimes infants fail to react because the jealousy situation is understimulating. Check whether the doll was appropriate. Was it lifelike? Did its features, especially the hair and skin color, match those of your infant? A doll that emits cute, cooing sounds is especially provocative. Another point to consider is whether the doll's sounds and your voice were heard. Make certain that your infant's hearing is not impaired. An infant whose ears are blocked due to sinus congestion may not be fully aware of your attention to the doll. Most important, consider whether your voice was sufficiently stimulating. Remember that the doll is lifeless. Therefore, unless a parent's voice is extremely warm and cheerful, infants will fail to detect what is going on. So don't worry about sounding silly or fake. Just put your heart into the act, and ham it up with as much playful affection and exaggerated sweetness toward the doll as possible. If anything triggers infant jealousy, it is the sound of a parent's voice.

Another way to detect jealousy is by seeing if an infant's reaction depends on whether jealousy is being induced by a parent or a stranger. If you have a neighbor or colleague willing to share in the assessment procedure, have her pay attention to the baby doll just as if she was the parent. Then assess whether your infant's reaction was more negative when jealousy was induced by the stranger or yourself. Such contrasts usually reveal that parent-induced jealousy is a more emotional and more distressing experience for infants.

Finally, since there is no way to predict an infant's reaction, there is no way to know if it is safe to induce jealousy using a real baby rather than a doll. Infants become jealous regardless of whether they have been provoked by a doll or a real baby. After all, toddlers have no idea, at least initially, that the situation is contrived and that the doll is only a fake. Jealousy responses can be extremely hostile, and much of your child's aggression will be directed toward the object of parental attention. A real baby can be placed in danger of being attacked by the infant, so for this reason, I don't recommend using a real baby to trigger jealousy, even on a second try. Although use of a doll to trigger jealousy is advantageous because it eliminates any worry over a baby being harmed by a jealous toddler, parents want to avoid creating confusion between dolls and humans. That's why the assessment should only be conducted two or three times, at most. And note that the assessment should progress only until the moment an infant gets the notion that the doll is not a real infant. At that point, the episode is over, even if it falls short of sixty seconds.

Before You Begin

Some parents are especially sensitive to jealousy. Parents can find themselves quite taken by a sense of triumph over proven love, resulting in their spontaneous outpouring of love in return for the deep-down-in-your-bones-*knowing*-you-are-loved feeling that comes from being coveted deeply. So before embarking on the assessment procedure, you might wish to step back for a moment and prepare yourself. Imagine how *you* will feel if your toddler explodes with anger. Think, too, about how you will feel if your toddler's jealousy response is only barely discernable. Also consider how you may react to discovering a discrepancy between jealousy levels provoked by yourself versus those provoked by your spouse. If you like, take a moment and jot down some of your thoughts and feelings about the event about to take place in your life. In sum, give some thought to the possibility that your toddler may not react as you expect, or wish, and to the chance that your own gut reaction may not match with the feelings you had anticipated.

Chapter Five

Hot, Warm, and Cool
Jealousy Temperaments

To help you interpret your infant's reaction to the preceding jealousy exercise, this chapter describes three levels of temperament:
hot, warm, and cool. For each level, it depicts both typical and
abnormal characteristics as they appear in one-year-olds. It also
shows you how to identify the signs—green, yellow, and red—
which can help you decide whether it's advisable to go ahead, proceed with caution, or pause before having another child.

Hot

Infants whose manner of expressing jealousy is intensely negative
are said to have hot temperaments. This level of jealousy has several distinctive qualities. First, "hot" infants react exceptionally
quickly. They will literally leap to their feet or burst out with a
shriek. They erupt instantaneously, as though the mere sight of
the doll acts like a trigger, igniting an emotional explosion. These
visceral reactions occur so spontaneously, they appear to be

released almost reflexively, as if happening in the absence of conscious thought and without any sign of being under voluntary control, let alone restraint.

Infants showing hot jealousy are also relentless, becoming distraught the moment the doll appears. Sometimes they will use a variety of different tactics for showing their displeasure, but they do not let up until the doll is taken away. Occasionally, an infant will briefly pause upon determinating—usually by poking the doll's eyes—that the doll is not a real baby. But the discovery rarely counts. Most hot-tempered infants are incapable of demonstrating any form of self-restraint, and will simply resume protesting until the doll is removed. Regardless of whether they understand that the doll is real or not, they seem to hate it so much, they just want to see it destroyed.

Hot jealousy is expressed through a style reflecting anger primarily. A highly charged level of energy and some physical aggression are at the heart of these responses. Some infants are so energized by jealousy, they seem to have strength beyond a level one would think possible in infants so young. Hostility is directed mostly toward the doll. Many infants grab the doll by the hair, yanking the head backward with one hand, while poking its eyes with the other hand. Less frequently, infants show aggression toward their parents, often by biting, pinching, or kicking. An infant's barrage on the parent or doll tends to be accompanied by some screaming and yelling directly at the parent, usually while in physical contact with the mother or father, and subsides only long enough to permit the infant to inhale.

Atypical Hot Responses

Difficulties in an infant's emotional development are revealed through the display of particular features of intense disturbance.

In some instances, upon noticing their parent's fussing over the baby doll, instead of reacting with anger, infants will freeze up. Imagine a twelve-month-old assuming the classic deer-in-the-headlights posture, with elbows and shoulders raised, a dropped jaw, and a bug-eyed, unblinking facial expression. A kind of panic reaction can follow. Some infants will pace around frantically, or just stand still and flap their elbows up and down, before suddenly making a break for the nearest door. Though showing clear signs of agitation and confusion, these infants will not get close enough to their parents to physically connect.

Less overwhelmed infants can put together a response suggesting anger, but their aggression will not be directed at the doll or the parent. Instead, these infants will direct their hostility toward the wall or the floor, usually using their hands or feet to pound on one of these surfaces. Such behaviors can be expressed so violently they are almost self-injurious. These intense reactions can escalate wildly into full-blown temper tantrums. Though there may also be considerable shouting with these vigorous outbursts, much of it is randomly directed, going in all directions except toward the parent. Sometimes, an infant's anger level starts off fairly subdued, apparently under control. Then, just as the jealousy episode is about to conclude, controls over emotion start to give way, and anger becomes unleashed instead of resolved. By the time the episode is over, the infant is heading toward a state of uncontrollable rage. Well after the doll is out of sight, some infants can be found still working up a fury. And again, no efforts are made to seek comfort from the parent or even to make physical contact.

Sadness is another response that can be expressed to an extreme level, and in a form that is outside the norm. Although some yelling is fairly common, true crying is unusual. When unaccompanied by any movement toward the parent, crying is exceptionally aberrant. In its most vehement form, sadness can be expressed through a panic cry. This consists of intense wailing, which springs up full blast, with no "warm-up" of any sort. One infant who demonstrated this level of emotional devastation made no effort to approach his mother. He just sat on the floor in the opposite corner of the room with his head thrown back and his face buried in his hands, howling nonstop.

Warm

Warm temperaments are evidenced by infants whose mode of expressing jealousy is moderately negative. This jealousy level includes an exceptionally broad range of behaviors, and most infants' responses will fall within its boundaries.

Generally, infants react quickly, but not instantaneously, usually within fifteen to thirty seconds. After that, protests will proceed at a stop-and-go pace. An infant will become distraught, then take a break from protesting, and then resume protesting. These breaks are key to an infant's ability to regulate his level of stress. As if unconsciously aware of being in a state of emotional turmoil, and at the same time recognizing limits to his ability to withstand such discomfort, an infant will make efforts to keep himself under control by using momentary intermissions for the purpose of emotional regrouping. Depending on an infant's tolerance for disequilibrium and his skill in managing stress, some infants take only fleeting breaks, while others take longer pauses from the business of protesting. The resulting ebb and flow in protests reflect the presence of both jealousy and coping skills, and a kind of balancing act aimed at keeping both in check. Thus, the on-off protest pattern indicates a balance, which is unique to each infant, between expressing jealousy versus coping with stress. Hotter infants lean more toward expressing their jealousy. Cooler ones put greater energy into controlling their jealousy.

A close look at behaviors exhibited during the intermission phase yields insights into infants' coping styles. As they stop protesting, most infants will also pull away from the source of pain. Infants do so usually by obscuring their parents from view, and there are innumerable ways in which this can be achieved. Some infants will turn their eyes or heads away, others will turn their backs to their parents, or sit crouched under the parent's chair. Still facing their parents, infants will sometimes close their eyes, or cover their faces with their hands, and in cases where an infant has access to a blanket or loose item of clothing, these can be draped over the infant's face.

Despite infants' attempts to cope with jealousy by recoiling from it, they are physically drawn to their parents for comfort and support. Occasionally, some will try to reconcile their needs to avoid jealousy and approach the parent by trying to accomplish both, more or less, at the same time. This results in an interesting, and not uncommon, pose, in which an infant may be standing close to his parent, even touching her, while twisted around so that he is turned away from her. Normally, in instances where an infant has something interesting to watch, this stance would not automatically suggest emotional upheaval. But infants can maintain this position for an entire minute, while staring at a completely blank wall. Other times, when a second adult is present, infants will look toward that person as if seeking new sources of support. These infants will sometimes look puzzled, as if searching the adult's face for clues to help guide their next move.

While regrouping, infants will often suck their fingers or thumbs, or they might chew on some piece of cloth. They will fiddle with their hair, or some part of their clothing, such as a buckle or shoelaces, and can appear quite nervous, especially if their movements are demonstrated repetitively. The toy that was brought along can serve as a source of comfort by helping an infant distract himself from jealous feelings. Infants will hug these toys, sometimes clutching, squeezing, or wringing them so forcefully they are almost torn apart. Although destructive, these comfort-seeking behaviors are not acts of hostility. Nor is such use of the toy a form of play. True playfulness consists of an infant's full engagement and would entail looking at the toy while exploring it with his hands, all the while appearing cheerful and calm. In instances where the toy is being used as a comfort item, an infant holds (and perhaps mangles) the toy while looking elsewhere and maintaining a facial expression suggesting engrossed interest in the parent, rather than the toy. The difference between play and comfort-seeking behavior is not immediately obvious. Comfort-seeking behaviors are easily discounted by parents expecting jealousy to be manifested by anger. The fact that an infant is not protesting vigorously does not mean that he is indifferent to the jealousy situation. An infant who needs to comfort himself, is an infant who is upset.

The protest phase of an infant's response is characterized by anger, sadness, or, more typically, some blend of these two emotions. Additional emotional expressions can be interwoven. Some infants show surprise or fear, especially during the initial moments of the episode. Brief looks of disgust, pain, and even contempt can also cross their faces. Whatever facial expression an infant displays, it is generally accompanied by whining and clinging to the parent. Whining can range from intermittent grunts to vigorous clamoring. Physical contacts with the parent can consist of one-handed tapping on a parent's toe, to two-fisted beating on the lap. Latching on to the parent's clothing is common, especially in infants still unsteady on their feet. More agile infants might use parents' clothing as scaffolding for helping them mount their parents' laps. In combination, these vocal and behavioral demonstrations of distress are geared toward expressing an infant's displeasure, and communicating such displeasure, clearly and directly to the parent. Even infants showing only mild pestering stay in close proximity to their parents almost half the time.

Contacts with the doll are infrequent. When they do occur, the infant is usually looking at the parent, rather than the doll. If the infant *is* looking at the doll while touching it, the contacts usually consist of swiping movements. Such efforts can be forceful, but are aimed at removing the doll from the parent's lap, rather than attacking it intentionally. Sometimes an infant will gain close access to the doll and figure out that it is not a real infant. Most will then back off, some with surprise or indignation at having been tricked, others with a giant wave of relief spreading across their little faces.

Atypical Warm Responses

Abnormal protest patterns in infants with warm temperaments are characterized by infants failing to approach their parents despite being in a state of disequilibrium. An infant might stomp around in circles, frenetically, occasionally brushing past the parent, as if unable to bring himself to actually make contact. Another might wander about aimlessly, looking lost, and then slump into a remote corner of the room and rock, or suck his thumb, or fidget with some fragment of clothing. One infant stood sucking his thumb and facing his mother from a safe distance. All the while, he rocked from one foot to the other, tipping sideways to the point of almost tottering over completely, while veiled from head to toe by a blanket. Then the blanketed little mound shuffled away.

Even if an infant is not openly crying, an expression of deep sadness, in combination with physical distance from the parent, is troubling. This response appears exceptionally irregular when the infant also makes no effort to communicate. As if afraid to draw any attention toward himself whatsoever, one infant just gaped while his mother fussed over the baby doll. As his mouth and shoulders drooped lower and lower, his eyes grew wider and wider and slowly welled up with tears. Yet this forlorn infant never took a step toward his mother, nor did he utter so much as a whimper.

Cool

Cool temperaments are indicated by behaviors suggesting only mild agitation. These infants seem to take their time catching on to what a parent is up to with the baby doll, and they dither around before making their way over to the parent. Once in proximity, their responses are intermittent rather than tenacious, and signs of displeasure are fleeting. Often, a cool-tempered infant is genuinely happy to see a baby. These infants are sociable and seem to like babies, even those receiving attention from their own mothers. Such friendliness puts a damper on jealousy and counteracts it effectively. Other infants are simply mellow to the point of being too phlegmatic to get worked up over anything, even jealousy.

Jealousy is detectable in these infants by drawing comparisons between their reactions to the doll episode versus those elicited in the picture book episode. The doll episode is more likely to elicit the knitting of eyebrows yielding a momentary look of anger, or at least apprehension, not quite apparent in the book episode. Sometimes a fleeting double take of surprise, a high-pitched yelp, a squinty-eyed look of suspicion, or clenched fists yield the only clues to the presence of jealousy. Often, reactions to the doll episode will incorporate curiosity with a slightly greater mix of caution. Whereas an infant's interest in the book usually goes along with his looking at the book, interest in the doll will be accompanied by infants looking somewhat more toward the parent. Some infants will go back and forth between offering friendly smiles to the doll and timid glances to their parents. Other infants seem to be communicating both friendliness and trepidation, simultaneously. In what is known as an appeasement smile, infants will hunch up their shoulders, squeeze their elbows into their sides, and scrunch up their eyebrows, while presenting a small, worried smile. In general, they will spend less time touching the doll than the book, and contacts with the parent will be more continuous during the doll episode. As a result, the doll episode will include somewhat greater physical contact and proximity to the parent.

Atypical Cool Responses

An abnormal protest pattern in cool-tempered infants is evidenced when the doll episode, in comparison with the book episode, fails to generate greater rates of contact with the parent and uncovers no discernable trace of distress in the infant. Generally, these infants keep to themselves and are at some distance, appearing unperturbed and content to simply go about playing in a cool, business-as-usual manner. They might be absorbed by the task of examining some detail of their shoes, or the room's furnishings, or the toy. They are not angry at the doll, nor are they friendly toward the doll. Neither stunned or numb, they simply appear emotionally flat and expressionless, as if they have mastered the task of tuning out the world to such a degree that they have no need to be a part of it or its ongoing events. Observing these infants, one gets the sense that such a level of disinterest suggests indifference, even apathy, toward the parent, and emotions so underdeveloped, that an infant is left looking as if he lives inside an emotional vacuum. In fact, some of these infants appear so cold and detached from their feelings, they seem to have no feelings at all.

It is important to recognize that in older toddlers and children, the very same sort of response could take on an entirely different meaning. A loss of exclusive access to a parent unveils numerous response styles, and these change considerably with age. A subdued reaction in an older child might be a positive sign. In a one-year-old, however, such languorousness does not represent self-restraint, maturity, virtue, independence, or selflessness. It suggests trouble.

Jealousy Temperaments

	Hot	Warm	Cool	Atypical
Onset	<15 sec	15–30 sec	>30 sec	never starts
Pace	on, nonstop until the doll is removed	on-off, mostly on	on-off, mostly off	never settles down, even after doll is removed
Emotional Content	angry	angry, sad, anxious	concerned, interested, friendly	no emotion, extreme sadness, or confusion
Positioning	physical contact with parent is continuous and forceful	physical contact with parent is continuous but *not* forceful	close to parent constantly, but only some physical contact	distant
Vocal Behavior	yelling	whining	occasional whimper	none, or crying

Now that you have led your own child through the jealousy exercise, consider the details of his reactions. Was the onset of his reaction fast or slow? Recall the give-and-take between protest and regrouping phases. How did he protest; how did he regroup? What did your infant do as the episode concluded? Could he calm himself down or was he just starting to wind up? Did he find out that the doll was not real, and how did this affect him? Were his reactions mostly signs of confusion or did he look angry, sad, or worried? Was there some indication of friendliness toward the baby doll? Most important, where did he place himself during the episode? Was he close enough to touch you, or was he beyond your reach? Did he make demands for your attention or was he subdued and withdrawn?

Red, Green, and Yellow

In the process of answering these questions, you will be determining whether your infant matches the profile of a hot-, warm-, or cool-tempered infant, and whether your infant's reaction falls within or beyond normal boundaries. Having done so, you are now in a position to use these insights to guide your next step in building your family. In fact, the knowledge you have gained from the brief test will help you make important decisions pertaining to your family's future. No two infants are exactly alike, and every infant's manner of expressing jealousy is unique. Some patterns are green lights, however, suggesting that an infant is likely to cope well with the arrival of a sibling. Others are red lights, which should alert parents to the possibility that an infant is emotionally in trouble. Still others are yellow lights, indicating that some caution is in order.

Red Light

Regardless of whether an infant shows a hot, warm, or cool jealousy temperament, atypical reactions to jealousy inducement are outside normal boundaries, and they are warning signs.

A distressed infant's failure to approach her parents for comfort is an indication that this is a troubled child. If a hot-tempered infant attacks the wall with his bare knuckles, or if a warm-tempered infant softly sobs at a distance, both children are indicating that they are disturbed but unwilling to cope by seeking parental support. If an infant is unaware of this option or fearful of using it, steps need to be taken to develop his awareness of the parent as an emotional resource, and to develop his trust in the parent's ability and willingness to provide such support. Infants should know that parents are there for them, even parents who appear preoccupied by another infant. No infant should react as if appeals to a parent are a waste of time because he has been replaced by another baby.

The cool-tempered infant's inability to approach or show distress are other clues that all is not well. Her carrying on at play, as though nothing out of the ordinary is transpiring, could suggest an underdeveloped level of jealousy or an underdeveloped parent-infant relationship. In either case, the infant is in need of tender attention. Unfortunately, this kind of dire situation can easily go unnoticed because, unlike heightened protests that immediately and loudly draw attention, dull reactions do not readily raise alarm. In other instances, the muted response is noted but mistaken for an easygoing nature. To the attentive parent or caregiver, however, the signs aren't difficult to read. Often, infants showing this distant and cold pattern are infants who operate on such a level habitually. These are infants who rarely cry, seek affection, or demand any form of attention, under any circumstances. To mistake low demands for attention as a sign of good adjustment is a serious oversight. Many experts would argue that an infant's underreaction is at least as serious as an overreaction. Detached and apathetic reactions are warning signs, as are shows of confusion, deep sadness, and withdrawal.

An infant showing any of these response styles is in no shape to take on the emotional burden of coping with the arrival of a sibling. In fact, it is quite likely that he would be ill-equipped to cope with any sort of stress and would later have difficulty bonding with a sibling. Parents who observe these response patterns in an infant are strongly urged to make the needs of this child a priority. The task of mending the relationship with this particular infant should take precedence over embarking on enlarging the family. Try the exercise again after making such efforts, and then see whether your infant's response now falls within one of the normal patterns.

Green Light

Infants showing warm or cool temperaments within normal boundaries appear well adjusted, and their parents should feel comfortable with the decision to proceed with plans to enlarge the family. These infants have intact relationships with their parents, and coping mechanisms are well in place for helping them withstand stress. Cool-tempered infants, in particular, are likely to show friendly reactions to a new infant in the household.

Yellow Light

Within normal boundaries, hot jealousy is a feature of healthy character development, but it is both good news and not-so-good news. The good news is that, despite exceptional levels of anger and hostility, these infants generally show no evidence of being emotionally troubled. In fact, evidence points in the opposite direction. Further, research on hot firstborns' reactions to the arrival of a sibling found that over time, most of these infants do a fine job of adjusting to a new baby.

Parents of hot-tempered babies should be forewarned, however, that in the short run these infants can be a handful. This doesn't mean that parents should put off having another child. Rather, parents simply need to proceed with some caution. When parents are aware of an infant's hot temperament, his vehement response to a newborn sibling's arrival should not come as a surprise or a disappointment, either to the infant or the parents. Also, parents should not feel discouraged or guilty for having failed at parenthood. Most likely, nothing could be further from the truth. Parents would do well to make extra efforts to ensure that their infants are emotionally prepared for a sibling's arrival. Become familiar with the material in the upcoming chapters, and keep in mind that paternal support at the time of a newborn's arrival will be especially critical to the child's adjustment.

On a less optimistic note, hot-tempered infants probably have some greater potential for developing unsafe levels of jealousy. Thus, these children need to be raised carefully. The arrival of a sibling is especially trying for a hot-tempered infant. How well he copes will depend largely on mothers' and fathers' patience and adeptness in managing the sibling relationship.

Nature versus Nurture

Knowing an infant's jealousy temperament helps foretell an infant's reactions to a newborn sibling's arrival; it can also provide some guidelines for predicting a child's long-term jealousy response style. Jealousy temperaments, though biologically based, are not governed by genes alone; parenting practices and life experiences shape the way in which innately based predispositions unfold. But even the best parenting can only go so far.

Jerome Kagan of Harvard University studied shyness, another feature of temperament. He found that infants are born with tendencies toward being timid or bold; in following these infants as they progressed through childhood, Kagan discovered that exceptionally bold infants can eventually become somewhat less bold, and exceptionally timid infants can eventually become less fearful. However, it is rare for a very shy infant to evolve into a very bold child, and conversely, very bold infants rarely turn out to be meek. Through particular child-rearing experiences, inherited proclivities can be moderated, but not overridden entirely.

Jealousy temperaments probably operate in a parallel fashion. As infants progress, their innate temperaments can unfold in either direction, so that jealousy can be become cooler or hotter. But it is unlikely that a cool-tempered infant will ever develop jealousy to the extent seen in hot-tempered infants. Conversely, hot-tempered infants will probably never turn out cool.

Summary

Jealousy temperaments can be classified as hot, warm, or cool.

- Hot-tempered infants show immediate, intense, and unrelenting anger.
- Warm-tempered infants show a mixture of anger, sadness, and anxiety, counterbalanced by coping behaviors.
- Cool-tempered infants react slowly, with a mixture of concern and friendliness.

A troubled infant can show any of these three levels of jealousy. In addition, however, these infants

- stay physically distant from the parent, and
- underreact by appearing apathetic, withdrawn, or sad to the point of crying, or
- overreact by becoming so upset, they are inconsolable.

Knowing an infant's jealousy temperament can provide you with realistic expectations of your firstborn's initial reactions and potential for adjusting to siblinghood. The jealousy exercise can help you determine whether your infant is ready for a new baby sibling.

Chapter Six

Jealousy Profiles of Infants

Mrs. King and Laura

Laura was more openly attached to her mother now. She followed her around, crawling as fast as she could. She stayed between her legs, leaning on them whenever her mother stopped long enough. Mrs. King had to step over her many times in a day. Occasionally she stepped on her.

Since she was able to say "bye-bye," "mama," and "dada," she mumbled "mama, mama" all day long. Any fears Mrs. King might have had about losing Laura with the weaning process were long since forgotten.

When Mrs. King picked up a friend's baby to hold, Laura stood up quickly by her lap. She began pushing at the other baby to shove her out. She tried to climb into her mother's lap in order to shove more effectively. Mrs. King teased her by continuing to hold the baby and by talking to him. Laura became frantic, whimpering and pulling on the baby's clothes and extremities to dislodge him. After he was put down, Laura sat huddled in her mother's lap, sucking her fingers, as if she did not dare leave her lap again. Mrs. King's thoughts turned to getting out of the house on her own—perhaps a job.

This passage was written by T. Berry Brazelton in one of his early and highly popular works, *Infants and Mothers*. The book tracks the first year's month-by-month development in three prototypic infants. The first infant is an example of an "active" baby, the second is a model of an "average" baby, and the third is a "quiet" baby.

Brazelton's description of Laura's reaction to the loss of exclusiveness is a vivid characterization of jealousy. It is also an excellent illustration of the failings of popular myths about jealousy. First, Laura is a firstborn child, and this display of jealousy reportedly takes place when she is only eleven months old. These observations point to the fact that jealousy is present in infants even before the first birthday and that it occurs even without the experience of displacement by a sibling. Second, Laura is upset by jealousy inducement despite *not* having been subjected to changes in her everyday life, affirming the argument that upsurges in jealousy are not precipitated merely by altered routines. Third, and most notably, Laura shows "frantic" levels of jealousy even though, of the three infants depicted in the book, she is the prototypical example of a "quiet" child. This, in particular, indicates that hot jealousy is not a feature of maltreated, maladjusted, ill tempered, overdemanding, or spoiled infants. Indeed, not only is Laura a calm and satisfied baby, she is also described as "openly attached" to her mother, suggesting that jealousy is born of love, not malice.

That a "quiet" child shows "frantic" jealousy illustrates a disparity in emotional development that can be partially explained as a phenomenon stemming from innately based features of temperament. Yet parental attitudes and behaviors also play a role in shaping jealousy, and the commentary on Mrs. King's feelings and actions provide some insight into these social influences. Of particular interest is Mrs. King's mixed reaction to her daughter's jealousy. On the one hand, Mrs. King was so drained by Laura's demandingness that she found herself dreaming of outside employment. On the other hand, this overtaxed mother was deliberately provoking, and actually prolonging, the very behavior she was lamenting. Despite Laura's tugging on the infant, in addition to her pushing, shoving, whimpering, and trying to climb onto her mother's lap, Mrs. King relentlessly persisted in taunting her distraught daughter by fussing over the friend's baby.

How can we make sense of such ambivalent behavior? Maybe Mrs. King's fears over "losing" Laura or Laura's love had not been fully resolved after all. Perhaps, during the period of transition from breast to bottle feeding, a time that often leaves mothers feeling a sense of loss, Mrs. King felt that Laura had become detached, not just physically, but emotionally as well. Thus, it may have been the case that Mrs. King needed some sign from Laura to reassure her that she was still loved by her infant daughter. And through the "quiet" Laura's pronounced, though irksome, jealousy, that is precisely what she heard.

Natalie and Me

Natalie was a pleasant and "easy" nine-month-old baby. Arriving to pick her up from the child care center where she spent two days a week, I peeked through the window and found Natalie in her crib, standing up and screaming, quite uncharacteristically. Natalie was straining forward, shaking the crib and obviously furious. After carrying on in this manner for a few moments, she abruptly closed her mouth, sat down, and started to play. Later, I was to learn that it had been the sight of Linda, the assistant teacher, caring for another child that had provoked Natalie's outburst. After thinking about what happened, I developed the impression that Natalie was attached to Linda. So, on the next occasion when Natalie was to spend the day in child care, I made a point of leaving Natalie with Linda. Subsequently, Natalie no longer protested when I departed, as she had in the past. Later, when asked if she was annoyed by Natalie's possessive outbursts, Linda said, "Yes," and then coyly added in a whisper, "but she is my favorite baby."

A comparable outburst was observed when Natalie was twelve months old and I took her to visit a newborn infant. In full view of Natalie, still strapped into a carrier and cheerfully engaged with a toy, I slowly and deliberately picked up the newborn baby as he began to cry. Instantaneously, Natalie's face contorted into a caricature of anger. Her eyebrows, normally positioned like quotation marks, bracketing her eyes, darted together into the shape of the letter V. Her lips parted into the form of a square, showing the place where canine teeth would be if she had had teeth. She thrashed her arms and legs, flushed a dark shade of red, and screamed. I was amazed, never having seen a young infant, especially the laid-back Natalie, quite so upset, and yet not shedding a tear. After a few seconds, I abruptly put the baby down. Equally abruptly, Natalie stopped screaming and resumed playing.

Dumbfounded by the intensity of this reaction, I repeated the event that had provoked it. This time Natalie demonstrated a level of distress that is indescribable. Her explosion threw the entire household into commotion. It began with Natalie's sisters, Alison and Lyndia, and ended with every member of the extended family screaming instructions, in tumultuous unison, directing me to put the baby down. Finally, Natalie's eyes began to well up with tears, as anger gave way to despair. I put the newborn down. This time Natalie was not easily placated. In fact, she refused to be removed from my lap for the remainder of the visit. Natalie was never to demonstrate such an outburst again, and I never behaved in such a way as to provoke it.

This pair of vignettes tells much about an infant's emotional development and relationships with adult caregivers. Clearly, her emotional tone reflected more than an immature and amorphous display of distress. Unmistakably, her tearless outburst repre-sented a well-defined expression of rage. The sheer intensity of Natalie's anger is dramatic evidence of the emotional clarity and depth of feeling available to an infant, even before her first birthday, and even in an otherwise "easy" baby. Since she was no more than twelve months of age, Natalie's rage was also totally unrestrained. By the time children reach the age of two years, they have begun to acquire some awareness of themselves and what they are doing. With the advent of self-consciousness, infants can watch themselves as they interact with the world. The intensity of Natalie's outburst reflects the emotional abandonment possible only where self-consciousness is still nonexistent, leaving all ener-gies available to be spent expressing anger.

Let's consider the communicative power of Natalie's jealousy. Words were not necessary in order for this infant to convey exactly what she wanted. I saw that Natalie was attached to Linda and decided to thereafter leave Natalie in Linda's care, rather than that of the head teacher. And Natalie, in turn, was happier. Indeed, prior to the outburst, it had seemed as though Natalie was not ready to receive care from any strangers. Her crying every morning as I departed seemed to suggest that Natalie felt unloved and uncomfortable in child care. But it was quite the opposite. In fact, Natalie was very comfortable in child care as long as she was in Linda's care. Had it not been for Natalie's jealous outburst, I would have withdrawn her from the center without ever knowing how contented my daughter felt in Linda's capable hands.

Because infants' separation protests and jealousy protests can look alike, they are easily mistaken for each other. If an infant fusses during a parent's presence in a child care setting, parents tend to automatically assume that the infant is saying, "Don't leave me" when, in fact, the infant might be trying to say, "Don't leave me with this particular caregiver; I want my favorite caregiver."

Some parents can even find it difficult to acknowledge that an infant *has* a favorite caregiver. Competition for an infant's love exists not only between mothers and fathers but also between parents and caregivers, nannies, grandparents, and babysitters. Natalie's jealousy attests to the fact that infants can be attached to more than one person. And, apparently, attachment relationships are not reciprocal. Alas, infants, not unlike some adults, expect to enjoy *receiving* love exclusively, even though they are not *giving* love exclusively!

Without doubt, Natalie is an infant whose temperament would be classified as hot. Her response, which might easily appear maniacal in an older child or an adult, bore no indication of pathology. To the contrary, except for these two jealous outbursts, Natalie was a placid, cheerful, and easygoing child. Doted on by her family and caregivers, Natalie was simply a child whose love was fierce, even as a baby. Over time, her pronounced love evolved into passionate and loyal devotion to her loved ones, her sisters, in particular. She turned out to be an exceptionally loving child, much adored by her family, at least in part because of her immeasurable ability to love them. As if the depth of Natalie's love drew deeper love in return, not only was Natalie Linda's favorite baby, she turned out to be everyone's favorite baby. Anyone with doubts that such a jealous baby could become such a loving sibling is encouraged to check out the photograph on page 172. The little girl with the magnificent eyes-squeezed-shut smile is Natalie at the age of three, with her beloved sisters, Alison and Lyndia.

Three Sets of Twins

Elsa Thomas and her twelve-month-old twins, Danny and Dorene, arrived on time for the medical school's jealousy study.

While Elsa took part in the preliminary interview, the twins kept the team of lab assistants fully occupied, and quite amused. The two were in constant motion, romping around the room, trying out every toy, flirting with each of the lab assistants, and, of course, pestering their mother every now and then. Above the din, Mrs. Thomas admitted that she sometimes felt tired, but that she was fortunate in having help from several family members, and a husband who was a great partner. She said too, that a tireless sense of humor, at least when it came to parenting, also came in handy.

Danny was the first of the twins to take part in the jealousy study. No sooner had the doll been placed on his mother's lap than Danny was right by her side. He stomped over, taking noisy marching steps, with his hands on his hips, his chin lowered to his chest, and a fierce-looking scowl on his face. He stayed there, yelling emphatically, until the doll was removed from his mother's lap. When it was Dorene's turn, her response was equally instantaneous, but different in emotional tone. She plopped down on the carpeted floor, and curled up so tight her head was in her lap. One hand was drawn over her face so that her elbows covered her eyes, and her other hand was placed over her mouth so she could suck her thumb. She stayed in that position, and rocked back and forth, for a few seconds. Then she ran to her mother, and began to whine and cling. Mrs. Thomas seemed to take this all in stride.

Andrea came to the lab with her daughters, Angie and Amy. The twins did not resemble each other. Angie was blond, and Amy was brunette. Andrea expressed some concerns over her ability to manage the twins, but was generally in good spirits. In the meantime, the twins seemed to be having a blast, fooling around with each other, creating much commotion, and loving every minute of being the center of attention. In the lab, Angie and Amy reacted to jealousy provocation by showing similar styles of response. Both approached Andrea immediately and clung to her, but Angie was much more upset. Clinging to Andrea, Angie whined and swiped at the doll and finally tried scrambling onto her mother's lap. Although Andrea insisted that she treated her twin daughters exactly alike, it turned out to be the case that Angie slept with her mother every night, while Amy slept with her grandmother.

Joanne appeared with her twins, Johnny and Jack, two hours late, disheveled and obviously exhausted. She reported that the twins were either out of control or crying, unless they were asleep, and that she felt depressed and overwhelmed most of the time. True to her description, managing the twins was a daunting task. Even the experienced research assistants had to call in reinforcements to handle the wild twosome. In the lab, it was Jack's turn first. He showed no reaction whatsoever when Joanne picked up the doll. Like other infants of depressed mothers, Jack kept his back to Joanne and amused himself by untying his shoelaces. Johnny, on the other hand, protested, whining at his mom. In the interview that followed, Joanne was asked if she treated the two children differently. Again, it turned out to be the case that the two infants were treated the same, except only one slept with his mother. This time, however, the infant who slept with his mother was the one who showed the minimal reaction, and the infant who slept with the grandmother was the one who showed some jealousy.

From these accounts, it appears clear that twins develop jealousy. Like second- or third-born children, twins develop jealousy despite never having had a parent's undivided attention. Although exclusiveness does not exist for these infants in reality, they do have the illusion of exclusiveness. "Egocentric" thinking, which allows an infant to see things only from his own point of view, might actually protect him from the grim fact of life that he is not the only baby receiving parental attention. Thus, each twin might *feel* like the number one infant, even though he isn't, and develop expectations of receiving preferential attention, and with it, jealousy.

Although jealousy emerges in twins, it does so quite differently in each individual infant. Danny and Dorene Thomas demonstrated contrasting response styles. Whereas Danny showed a fierce reaction, Dorene showed fearfulness. Danny's show of aggression and Dorene's show of timidity together are notable examples of gender-stereotyped behavior. As in other instances where infant responses match neatly with traditional sex roles, it is tempting to assume, but difficult to prove, the existence of a biological basis for disparities between male and female jealousy.

Angie and Amy showed parallel styles of expressing jealousy. Was the commonality rooted in similarities of genetic makeup or fairly equivalent experiences in upbringing? Though similar in tone, their responses were at distinct intensity levels; Angie's protests were of a greater magnitude. The difference could be an outcome of subtle differences in treatment at home. Perhaps Angie's greater jealousy is a reflection of her greater attachment to her mother; the two shared a bed, sleeping arrangements that afforded greater physical contacts and affection, not quite so available during the hectic day.

Differences between jealousy levels of Johnny and Jack were also linked with sleeping arrangements. Tellingly, however, the pattern was reversed. This time, greater jealousy was seen in the infant who did *not* sleep with his mother. This contradictory pattern appears to be a reflection of the emotional climates of infants' homes. Greater access, as in sharing a bed and more "quality time" spent with a high-functioning, nondepressed mother like Andrea is a boon to the mother-infant relationship. On the other hand, if a mother is depressed and unresponsive, like Joanne, then less contact with a child may be best in the short run, especially if other loving and more functional adults are available.

Unlike mothers of firstborn singletons, mothers of twins become well acquainted with the phenomenon of early jealousy. Perhaps their lesser enjoyment of this early form of sibling rivalry, for whatever reason, is one factor contributing to the better control of jealousy often seen in twins.

Three Depressed Mothers and Their Infants

One-year-old Monica was gayly carried into the medical school laboratory and grandly presented to the researchers by her grandmother, Mrs. Valle, a large, talkative woman with a loud voice. Monica's mother, Maria, trailed behind them, lugging the baby bag, a stroller, her mother-in-law's handbag, as well as the baby's odds and ends, including a sweater that was unnecessary in the summer heat, a sunhat Maria refused to wear, shoes that had fallen off the baby's chubby feet, and an extra pacifier or two. Maria's downcast eyes, barely audible voice, and wispy frame were in sharp contrast to Mrs. Valle's substantial features. While Maria completed a number of forms, Mrs. Valle proudly tended to Monica who seemed quite accustomed to being lavished with cheerful attention by her grandmother. Mrs. Valle answered most of the questions in the interview that followed, with Monica happily bouncing on her lap. But sullen Maria provided only laconic responses or she just sat back, in silence, and gazed out the window at nothing in particular.

Maria didn't perk up until she was presented with the doll. With some coaxing, Maria began to talk to the doll, softly and nervously. She stroked the doll's hair and pretended to play pat-a-cake. Then louder, but still with a quiver in her voice, she spoke up and playfully chatted about the doll's pretty features, as she caressed the doll, awkwardly but affectionately. She kept up the halting chatter for a few more seconds, until the moment when her daughter's protests broke out in the form of several loud shrieks accompanied by furious grabbing at the doll. In that very same instant, Maria spontaneously burst into a radiant smile. Wide-eyed with awe, it was as though this young mother had suddenly come to life.

When it was time to leave, all the baby paraphernalia had been packed up. But this time Maria carried Monica, while grandmother toted the bag, bottles, clothes, pacifiers, stroller, and handbag.

Penny was a seriously obese young woman. She wandered into the lab alone, sat down on the sofa, and appeared to go to sleep. A few minutes later, she was followed in by her boyfriend, Jake, hollow-eyed and scrawny. Finally, little Pete straggled in by himself, carrying his bottle. Penny would not cooperate in the interview and appeared so utterly unresponsive, the researchers conjectured that she must have been heavily sedated. Pete kept himself busy with the toys. He made no effort to make contact with the lab assistants, or even Penny or Jake, for anything, even routine care, and appeared not to notice when Penny briefly left the room to use the restroom. Anyone looking at these three individuals would have assumed that they were total strangers.

But once the video camera began rolling it turned out, much to the crew's astonishment, that Penny had a clear voice. She held the doll gently and verbalized sweetly. No sooner had the crew recovered from the shock of seeing Penny act human, when they found themselves again gaping. This time, it was Pete's protests that had them stunned. It certainly was not a drastic reaction, or even a moderate response. Actually, it consisted of a few moments of stillness, followed by a sad, pathetic little whimper from the opposite corner of the room, directed toward the wall. Still, it was a shock to realize that this infant had been paying enough attention to his mother to even notice what she was doing, let alone get upset. But the most unexpected event was yet to come.

When the episode ended, Penny stood up and walked across the room in slow motion to where Pete stood whimpering. She squatted down to Pete's level and with exaggerated tenderness, picked him up. Positioning one arm beneath his head and the other under his knees, she cradled him like a newborn infant, rocking him softly, from side to side, silently. Absorbed inside his mother's bosom, Pete simply went limp as a rag doll, as if affection was so foreign to him that hugging his mother in return was not an option within his grasp. This woman, by far the most depressed and unresponsive mother that had ever entered the lab, now expressed a most lavish show of affection over a bizarrely wilted toddler. Then Penny put Pete down abruptly, turned around, and walked out of the room. With that, she slipped into her former state of solitary aloofness, and once inside the emotional fog, stayed there for the remainder of the visit. Later, the threesome left just as they had come in, one by one, oblivious of each other and everyone around them.

Nina and her daughter, Nickie, entered the lab together, quietly. Nina answered all of the interviewer's questions in a polite whisper, using a minimum of words. Despite her reluctance to elaborate on any of the items, and little evidence of any interest in the study, it was clear from her articulate speech and a certain air of demureness, that this was an educated and intelligent woman. Throughout the preliminary procedures, Nickie showed no curiosity toward the toys that were scattered about the room. She ignored the playful bids of the research assistants, ready with bubble wands to entertain infants whose mothers were preoccupied with the interview. Whatever had to be done for Nickie was carried out by her mother, methodically and wordlessly. Apart from these chores, there was no contact between Nina and Nickie. Immaculately outfitted in pink stockings, a frilly dress, and matching bows in her hair, Nickie just sat on the sofa next to her mother, without moving or uttering a sound, like an exquisite little doll with big eyes and a vacant stare.

When Nina was presented with the doll in the jealousy study, she softly and sweetly began to chatter and coo. She easily kept up the affectionate prattle without needing encouragement or guidance. Nickie observed her mother for a moment. She then lay down on the carpet, flat on her back, in the middle of the room, put her thumb in her mouth, and continued to gaze at her mother with the same blank stare. Except for an occasional eye blink, Nickie remained locked in this position right up until the end of the episode. When the doll was removed from her mother's lap, Nickie stood up, took two short steps toward her mother, and then stopped. At this point, both Nickie and Nina froze, a yard apart from each other, grimly looking at each other's feet.

From their responses on the interviews and various question-naires, as well as their demeanor, it is clear that the three mothers described in these vignettes were extremely unhappy women. Their sad recalcitrance notwithstanding, each complied fully with the instructions and did their best to provoke jealousy. In Penny's case, this was an exceptionally remarkable feat. What level of effort it must have taken for this woman to be dredged from her deep misery is hard to imagine. One can only surmise that the appeal of an infant's jealousy represents an incredible draw. And to these emotionally starved women, the draw of jealousy seemed to have represented something especially powerful.

Despite similarities in the mothers' conduct, their infants' reactions differed markedly. The most pronounced reaction came from Monica. Although Maria was out of sync with the goings-on of family life, her nervous anticipation of Monica's reaction divulged some emotional involvement. It also foretold her infant daughter's reactivity. Grandmother was a key factor in the equation. Though somewhat overbearing, she had obviously invested a great deal in Monica. And some of the love that she had given Monica was available for Monica to give her mother. The positive outcome of this transfer of love was evidenced when Monica's outburst of jealousy triggered an effusion of joy in her depressed mother. Maria's profound emotionality and her touching gratitude afterward disclosed an awakening, perhaps for the first time, to her daughter's love. This was an instance where an infant's hot jealousy temperament was advantageous to family cohesion. Monica's display of hot jealousy was all it took to jolt Maria into the realization that she was loved, and into accepting motherhood.

The outlooks for Pete and Nicki were less sanguine. The indications of jealousy in Pete bespoke at least some connectedness with the remote Penny. However, keeping himself at a distance and directing his mournfully pallid protests at the wall, instead of his mother, were obvious clues to weaknesses in the mother-infant relationship. What was this infant to make of his mother's over-indulgent response? Coming from a habitually responsive and affectionate mother, such a doting reaction might not have made much of an impression. But coming from a mother usually no warmer than a mannequin, this level of warmth, which Pete probably had not experienced since he was a newborn, must have provided a striking lesson in how to evoke loving attention. Surely, he had learned a new strategy for being guaranteed love. Unfortunately, his strategy lay in jealousy, and only in jealousy. For some families a show of jealousy is the one and only technique for kindling love, and it remains so throughout life.

If Pete was the most chilling case, Nickie was the saddest. Her flat and lethargic reaction was a pitiful sight. The utter lack of communication between Nicki and Nina, let alone anything even briefly suggesting affection or joy, marked severely blunted emotional development and disclosed a relationship devoid of love. In this depressed couple, there seemed only loneliness and despair.

PART THREE

The Second
Love Triangle

Chapter Seven

Closely Spaced Siblings

My boys are what were once called Irish Twins; that is, I had them less than two years apart and far too close together for most people's comfort. . . . I did this because I had a deep and enduring belief that two children born less than two years apart would become boon companions and lifelong friends, despite all the evidence I'd seen to the contrary. But this is indeed what happened. Quin could not remember life before Christopher, and Christopher had never had a life without Quin.

—Anna Quindlen, *Siblings*

STRATEGY FOUR in preventing sibling rivalry calls for a look at age spacing between children. What age difference works best for dampening jealousy and, even more important, cultivating friendship between siblings?

Couples consider a variety of issues in the process of deciding when to have a second child. Besides factoring in a mother's health and family finances, parents think about the emotional impact a second child will have on a firstborn child. Parenting experts have contributed to this aspect of the decision-making process by offering views on what they consider ideal spacing between children. In recent years, widened age differences have become increasingly

popular. It is now common to hear psychiatrists, psychologists, and physicians advise gaps of three to four years between births. These child experts base their recommendations on several considerations, many of which are set on some shaky ground.

Why Wait

Advocacy for wide spacing is based primarily on concerns over the status of a firstborn's relationship with his primary caregiver, what we call the mother-infant relationship, or bond. Many experts feel that this relationship should be solidified before being tested by the arrival of a second child. The rationale here is that the longer a parent-child relationship remains exclusive, or at least has the appearance of exclusiveness, the greater the chance it will gather sufficient strength to withstand a second child's intrusion. In other words, the longer an infant has his mother's undivided attention, the better are his chances of emotional survival.

This impression stems partly from a related concept: that wide spacing is conducive to *physical* survival. In fact, there is undeniable evidence that an infant's physical health, and even his chances of surviving infancy, are enhanced by exclusive parental attention. This evidence comes from studies conducted in the third world, which, tragically, show trends linking maternal starvation to infant mortality. Clearly, if a mother is suffering from malnutrition, the probability of her firstborn infant's survival is dramatically improved if she delays a subsequent pregnancy and thereby devotes all of her physical resources to her firstborn child exclusively. Under extreme conditions of hardship, a mother's resources are so tapped out by one child that she is incapable of nurturing a second infant through pregnancy and a period of breastfeeding.

Fears of being unable to physically sustain an infant are profoundly embedded in the nature of motherhood. Remarkably, these worries endure even in cultures where malnutrition affects very few. Every physician is familiar with the mother who is convinced that her infant is failing to thrive even when he is not in the least underweight. Every breastfeeding mother knows the self-doubt and worry that comes from irrational fears over whether an infant, even a plump infant, has had enough food. Although Western culture has adopted a preference for thinness, and one so pronounced that it borders on obsession, we still love chubby babies. How we adore round and rosy cheeks. Those cheeks are kissed, caressed, and beheld with such pleasure that even the most neurotic parent takes comfort in them. Long after an infant has grown up, and has probably been on and off several weight-loss diets herself, her mother will still gaze at the old baby photos and thrill at the sight of those pudgy cheeks, those symbols of her baby's vigor.

So ingrained are a mother's agonies over whether she can supply her infant with enough physical sustenance, her concerns actually spill over into yet another source of anguish—worry over whether she can supply adequate levels of emotional sustenance. This parallel pattern of concern centers on whether an infant's emotional survival is threatened by a new baby arriving and then demanding his share, or even a greater share, of the mother's emotional resources. So, even if a mother feels confident in her ability to support the physical and nutritional demands of more than one infant, doubts will still linger over whether she can support more than one infant's emotional needs.

It isn't easy for even the most confident parents to erase these sorts of self-doubts. If only we could reckon with such worry through a process as uncomplicated as taking the measure of a baby's weight or the fullness of his cheeks. Instead, to get a reading of an infant's emotional vigor and parental abilities to sustain him emotionally, parents have looked to parenting experts. Infancy researchers have examined infants' emotional fortitude by trying to measure the strength of the attachment bond between parents and infants. Traditionally, child development researchers have relied on a method known as the Strange Situation, which was developed by Mary Ainsworth over two decades ago. This half-hour laboratory procedure entails placing an infant in an unfamiliar setting and then observing him while alone, while with an unknown adult, and while with a parent, usually the mother. The security of a mother-infant relationship is evaluated on the basis of an infant's reactions to his mother's repeated departures and reentries, his attitude toward the strange environment, and his manner toward the new adult. An infant is rated as securely attached if he shows preferences for his mother over the stranger, curiosity toward the new surroundings, and contentment in general. Also, secure infants are upset by their mothers' departure, and upon her return, they approach her for comfort and are soothed by her warm reception.

For psychologists who study early child development, the Strange Situation has revealed myriad insights into the benefits of secure attachment. Compared with their insecure peers, securely attached one-year-olds have later been rated by preschool and kindergarten teachers as more popular, resilient, and independent. They are more playful, affectionate, and cooperative. Being less fussy and difficult, they have fewer behavior problems. They also show more frequent and more mature behaviors with peers. Their social overtures seem to go over better. Secure toddlers are better at sharing, making friendly gestures, and then keeping a social exchange going. When stressed, they are less likely to fall apart and more likely to bounce back. Greater trust and friendliness toward new adults has often been reported. In addition to exhibiting superior social competence, these toddlers demonstrate more optimal intellectual and achievement-related behaviors. They are more willing to try something new, and when faced with a challenge, they are less likely to give up. They show more interest and curiosity in new endeavors, and greater eagerness to explore and ponder over obstacles. They are more focused on tasks and willing to go along with instructions. Not surprisingly, on a whole variety of problem-solving tasks, secure children out-perform insecure children. Last, but not least, secure toddlers are also more playful and loving toward their baby siblings.

So who are these infants so fortunate as to find themselves in securely attached relationships? Some debate exists over how attachment happens. In the United States, studies find that secure attachment is associated with infants receiving nurturant, atten-tive, and nonrestrictive parental care. Studies also emphasize the importance of parental responsiveness. Others pinpoint the role of sensitivity. Still others see parental warmth as playing the key role. And in some cases, investigators have focused on the absence of certain undesirable parenting behaviors, such as overstimulation, understimulation, badly timed and erratic patterns of stimulation, and rejection. Although researchers are not entirely in agreement on precisely which factor, or cluster of factors, account for secure attachment, most recognize that, in large part, it has to do with some aspect of parenting behavior.

In the meantime, after more than two decades of research on the origins and advantages of secure attachment, studies have unveiled no evidence to suggest that these have anything to do with an infant receiving exclusive parental care. Despite controversies over the importance of various features of early parental attention, including warmth, responsiveness, sensitivity, and timing, there is little to support the notion that an infant needs to receive any of these forms of treatment within the context of an exclusive parent-infant relationship. In fact, where studies have attempted to capture the critical ingredient of secure attachment, exclusiveness is hardly ever even considered. In parallel, wide spacing, which entails greater access to exclusive parental attention, has not been shown to be advantageous to secure attachment. Nor have there been studies suggesting that wide spacing is advantageous to the sibling relationship. After so many years, and hundreds, perhaps even thousands, of studies inquiring into the quality of the parent-infant relationship, it is remarkable that the value of exclusiveness or wide spacing are rarely even addressed, let alone found critical, to an infant's psychological adjustment.

Instead, research indicates that an attachment bond is discernable by the time an infant is approximately twelve months of age, and most of the time its status remains constant thereafter. An infant who is insecurely attached by age one will probably remain so. Studies have yielded no evidence suggesting that an insecure infant will eventually "outgrow" his insecure status simply with the passage of time. Time simply doesn't guarantee that things will get better. And so, waiting for the attachment relationship to solidify before introducing an additional child makes some sense up until an infant's first birthday. After that, simply waiting for time to pass is waiting for nothing.

Of course, attachment status has been known to fluctuate. When this occurs, however, it does so not merely with the passage of time. Destabilized attachment status happens as a consequence of significant life changes, such as alterations in child care arrangements. In such cases, transitions in attachment status are as likely to involve insecure infants now becoming secure, as secure infants now becoming insecure, with the direction of change depending on the quality of care. Now comes the big question: Does the arrival of a sibling predispose a child to destabilized attachment status? If so, would such destabilization necessarily cause harm, incurring transitions from secure to insecure attachment?

Margot Touris and her colleagues at Loyola University set out to answer this question by assessing the attachment status of nineteen-month-old toddlers before and after the arrival of a sibling. Compared with a control group of non-siblings (who had not undergone a transition to siblinghood), the sibling group experienced more changes in attachment status. Notably, however, the transitions were as likely to be positive as negative. The big plus from this study is the discovery that with the arrival of a baby sibling, toddlers often actually end up *more* secure than before. As a number of classic studies showed, the arrival of a sibling poses a challenge, and while some children are beaten by it, others rise to the occasion. Firstborns sometimes take to their newly acquired status as the older child by showing new self-reliance in matters such as dressing, toilet use, and feeding, even volunteering to give up their "babyish" bottles, and by contentedly entertaining themselves. Thrust into the role of older sibling, these children adapt by becoming more independent, more mature, and in a healthy way, more grown-up.

Finally, if it were true that greater amounts of exclusive parental attention are beneficial to an infant's emotional well-being, then twins should be in especially poor emotional shape. After all, compared with closely spaced siblings, twins receive less exclusive parental attention, and they certainly, receive much less than widely spaced siblings. Yet, instead of finding that twins are prone toward insecure attachment, scientific inquiry into the emotional life of twins has uncovered no evidence that these children are socially compromised by never having been in an exclusive relationship with parents. Just as closely spaced siblings are not worse off than widely spaced siblings, twins are not worse off than closely spaced siblings.

To the contrary, there is ample evidence suggesting that twins are happy and well-adjusted individuals. Parenting books on the topic of raising twins are plentiful and enthusiastic about the outcomes of raising infants in pairs. This is really quite extraordinary when considering that twins may lose out on more than just exclusiveness. Since parents of twins are on double duty, in addition to giving their infants less exclusive attention, necessary shortcuts in care would seem to entail also providing them with less absolute attention. Not only will a twin receive no exclusive attention, but compared with a singleton, he might even receive less attention altogether. Nevertheless, the emotional development of twins is just fine.

Equally significant, parents of twins will be the first to admit that the amount of work entailed in raising twins is enormous. Yet they seldom mention regrets over having twins. During the past decade, I have polled numerous sets of twins and their mothers. Most of the time, when asked whether they would elect to have twins if they had to do it all over again, mothers of twins opted in favor of having twins over singletons. In cases where twins had been raised in families that included a third sibling, mothers qualified their opinions. Especially in instances where there had been several years between births, mothers would recall that raising twins had been easier and more gratifying than raising singletons. Some even suggested that, rather than suffering from a scarcity of attention, the twins actually benefited from the companionship of a sibling and from being spared excessive parental hovering. In parallel, twins themselves reported that they enjoyed the experience of being and having a twin sibling, and they, too, opted in favor of twinship, if given the choice. Apparently, twins themselves seem to feel that missing out on exclusive parental attention is not a major loss.

Waiting for Reason

Aside from an overblown belief in the value of exclusive parental attention, another source of justification for wide spacing has been generated by notions that a child with more advanced cognitive abilities will be better able to withstand a newborn's arrival. Many feel that older children, because of their greater intellectual maturity, are in a better position to understand, and therefore be spared, experiencing jealousy. Moreover, parents think that, being older and smarter, these children have greater potential for deriving benefits from parental initiatives to cushion the impact of a sibling's arrival. And such initiatives take many forms.

In recent years, parenting experts have promoted various rather formal instructional practices to prepare firstborn children for jealousy. Parents are advised to engage their firstborn children in discussions about events way in the future, like changes in household routines, mothers' eventual hospitalization, and her preoccupation with a baby, and events way in the past, like the firstborn's own early infancy. Discussions are to include frank treatments of abstract issues such as expected feelings, mixed reactions, dealing with displacement and disappointments, as well as explanations of complex biological processes such as conception and fetal development. Parents are told that such discussions should be complemented by reading storybooks and by role playing through visits to see friends who have babies, to the obstetrician, and to the maternity ward, and through participation in sibling preparation courses. Additionally, some authorities have suggested the benefits of acquiring pets.

One major drawback to these suggestions is that they require the two- or three-year-old toddler to comprehend emotions the way adults do. But emotions, especially multifaceted ones like jealousy, are abstract concepts. We cannot see them or touch them; we can only feel them. Research by Susan Harter and her colleagues at the University of Denver shows that preschoolers experience conflicting feelings, but their abilities to understand and talk about them will lag way behind. A child will have to be six or seven years old before understanding that it is possible to have more than one emotion at a time, and even then he'll find this conceivable only in situations where two emotions are similar in nature. So while feeling happy and proud might make sense, the notion that one can feel both happy and sad will not be so easy to comprehend. To illustrate just how complicated mixed emotions are to young children, Paul Harris at Oxford University offers a six-year-old's explanation of dual-faceted situations:

> *Interviewer:* The other day, I was talking to two children. One said that you could feel happy and sad, both at the same time. The other child said that was silly: you couldn't feel happy and sad at the same time. Who was right do you think? Can you feel happy and sad at the same time or not?
>
> *Six-year-old child:* No, because you haven't got two heads— you haven't got enough brains.

Also too young to get the hang of mixed emotions, a seven-year-old offered this:

> *Interviewer:* Do the sad feelings mix together with the happy ones or stay separate?
> *Seven-year-old child:* Stay separate.
> *Interviewer:* When Bill is happy do the sad feelings go away?
> *Seven-year-old child:* Some part of his body is happy and some part of his body is sad.

By age nine or ten, a child can be aware of the simultaneous presence of two entirely different feelings, but only if they are generated by two separate events. For example, a child of this age can understand that it might be possible to feel unfortunate over being ill, while also feeling fortunate over the chance to miss school. The last step, in which children comprehend that two dissimilar feelings can result from just a single event, requires the still more advanced thinking that comes with preadolescence.

Young toddlers can certainly *feel* jealousy's love and anger at the same time. Often, a two- or three-year-old will be cross with his parents while enthralled by a new baby. But it is highly un-likely that any insight into such mixed reactions will be gleaned by having these concepts explained—some time way in ad-vance—via lectures, storybooks, or role playing. To comprehend that a sole occasion, such as the birth of a sibling, can provoke the simultaneous and contradictory feelings of joy and resentment is well beyond the grasp of a two- or three-year-old toddler. Based on the available research, the reasoning skills of an eleven-year-old may be what it takes to understand jealousy.

As Michael Lewis of the Robert Wood Johnson Medical School at the University of Medicine and Dentistry of New Jersey points out, young children learn to understand emotions not by being told about them but by feeling them and then making connections between their feelings and co-occurring events. Linkages between feelings and events, or emotional scripts, are evident in children as young as three, who can link the experience of being lost, say, in a department store, with the feeling of fear. Similarly, he can match up the experience of eating ice cream with the feeling of pleasure. He cannot, however, connect feelings to events that he has never experienced. Hence, it is very unlikely that a child has any way of developing a script for jealousy without having gone through the experience of losing exclusive parental attention. And so, describing the feeling of jealousy to a preschooler who has never felt jealous might be about as useful as describing the color blue to someone who is blind.

Emotion research still has a lot of gaps. More studies are needed to fully unravel the process through which children formulate some understanding of jealousy. Certainly, it is important for a toddler to be prepared for a newborn's arrival. And, as the next chapter shows, it *is* possible for a toddler, even a young preverbal toddler, to be prepared for this emotional hurdle. There is no evidence, however, to suggest that preparation via verbal methods of instruction are helpful to young firstborns. Based on the available research on children's understanding of emotion, it is highly unlikely that such evidence will ever be uncovered.

Books are still great for toddlers, wonderful even if jealousy isn't the main topic. And visits to see family, friends, and neighbors are fine, although it is quite unlikely that an outing to the hospital is going to be worth more than a trip to the zoo. On the other hand, visits that include babies have been known to backfire. One classic study reported that a four-year-old child was devastated upon discovering that his newborn sibling did not look anything like the adorable eight-month-old he had been shown earlier. Similarly, sibling preparation classes may not be completely benign for young toddlers. While incapable of understanding the verbal content, three-year-olds can pick up on the stern atmosphere and sense of foreboding that are sometimes subtly and inadvertently conveyed by these programs.

Alternatives

Belief in the value of exclusive parental attention is overrated and exaggerated, and probably as irrational as worrying over whether a plump baby is malnourished. Nevertheless, parents cling to fears that their firstborns might be threatened by being deprived of years of exclusive parental care. Similarly, parents think they would be cheating if they failed to comply with recommendations for wide spacing, or if they failed to prepare their firstborns through formal, albeit impossible, methods of preparation. Certainly, these notions are upheld with the kindest and most generous of intentions, and, on the surface, they seem harmless enough. In fact, they appear so harmless that, despite the absence of any proof that they work, authorities feel comfortable advocating them wholeheartedly. Unfortunately, few recognize that there are hazards involved in adhering to these beliefs unquestioningly.

A minor downside is that well-intentioned parents' time and energies are wasted on some impractical measures for preparing firstborns. Of greater significance is that many of the recommendations are so impractical they verge on being elitist. Who but a car owner would think of bringing a toddler along on doctor visits? The whole idea of such visits is even less feasible if a pregnant mother is going to use public transportation in order to see a doctor whose office is located in a public hospital or clinic. Unlike private physicians' offices, clinics may not have the staff, space, or equipment necessary for accommodating lively toddlers, to say nothing of the amount of time a family might have to spend in one of these less-than-optimal waiting rooms. And if the mother has more than just one toddler in tow, the task of taking children to see the obstetrician has to be daunting. Similarly, the idea that a pet could be of help to a toddler's adjustment might not be so tempting to a mother who does not have extra help on hand for the purpose of taking the dog for walks or cleaning up after it or and training it. The unspoken message in these kinds of impractical recommendations is that preparedness is a privilege, reserved for middle-class mothers with cars, private physicians, and hired help.

While conveniently ignoring the needs of less-privileged mothers, proponents of formal methods for preparedness also ignore differences between children. As we know by now, jealousy temperaments differ widely. A hot-tempered toddler is quite unlike a cool-tempered one. By overlooking the broad temperamental disparities between children, we can expect to find many firstborns subjected to material that is entirely inappropriate. A cool-tempered child who is friendly and sociable probably needs less preparation than a hot-tempered child. Arguably, she already is as prepared as she ever will ever be. On the other hand, a hot-tempered child may need to be more carefully and intensively nurtured, and his greater needs cannot be met unless they are first recognized. Without addressing a child as a unique individual and taking his distinct jealousy temperament into account, it is unlikely that the usual preparatory steps can be of much use, and they may even be counterproductive.

The major drawback to popular recommendations for sibling preparation cuts across social class and temperamental differences between children. While being given advice that is often misguided and unproven, parents are also told it is their duty to provide their firstborn children with some kind of formal preparation. This creates a dilemma for them. On one hand, parents feel obliged to comply with authorities espousing three- to four-year age differences between siblings, but on the other, many sense that the heavily promoted methods for preparing firstborns are often ineffective with toddlers as young as two to three years of age. Hence, parents face two choices.

The first option is for parents to use the recommended suggestions for preparing their toddlers, and to fail. Despite knocking themselves out trying to adhere to recommendations, parents often find that their firstborns *are* jealous, which leaves them disappointed in themselves, or in their children, or both. Wondering where they could have gone wrong, parents are at a loss in managing their children's behavior. Instead of getting off to a reasonably good start, feeling confident and optimistic, at the outset, they feel deflated and exasperated, and a negative cycle of events is set in motion. Obviously, the problem, in these instances, is that the families have been set up for failure.

The second option is for parents to adhere to the recommended suggestions, more or less unfailingly, but with *older* firstborn children. While deeply committed to the idea that their firstborns have to be prepared through some formal treatment, these parents also recognize the limitations of their firstborn two- and three-year-olds. They realize that young children, and late bloomers in particular, cannot be expected to master the concepts inherent in the recommended measures. And so parents wait until their firstborns are older before introducing formal methods of preparation. This of course, entails a delay in having a second child. For the sake of having better-prepared firstborn children, parents wind up with age spacing that is beyond the recommended age difference of three to four years. In fact, such well-intentioned concern often results in very wide spacing, and that comes with a price.

Preventing Sibling Rivalry
Strategy Four

If an infant's performance in the jealousy exercise reveals that the stage is set for a healthy adjustment to a sibling's arrival, it means that mothers and fathers have nurtured an emotionally health infant and there is no reason to delay in having another child.

The quick addition of a next-born child, within two to three years, is optimal because it encourages companionship, thus setting up the best chance for cultivating *the* antidote for sibling rivalry: sibling friendship and, along with it, family unity.

Costs of Wide Spacing

Most parents choose to have more than one child, a decision driven by a number of considerations, foremost of which is the desire to give a firstborn child a companion and playmate. Young toddlers form friendships, and because relationships with young peers are less mature than those between adults, toddlers are unable to put their feelings into words. But their behaviors show that they certainly prefer to play with children over adults, and they can identify special children whom they enjoy, in particular. They give them more attention, more play invitations, sweeter hugs, bigger smiles, more talk, even compliments. And they receive the same in return. Toddlers enjoy spontaneity, intimacy, and emotional rewards through friendship. They even show sympathy and warmth when their little chums are down.

Early peer friendships can be innocent and warm, but they are not perfect. Adults seem particularly inclined to romanticize notions about children's early friendships and to ignore the reality that young pals who spend time together sharing also spend time squabbling. To most obervers, it is quite obvious that friends can be jealous of each other. Young friends compete and they have fights. These are not big fights, and they are quickly resolved. Clearly, though, early friendships include rivalry as well as resolution. Finally, friendship is not automatic. Friendships between children grow if the children are compatible playmates. According to Willard Hartup of the University of Minnesota, usually these are children who like taking part in similar types of activities.

Like peer friendships, sibling friendships are not automatic. When they do evolve, studies show that they begin with the advent of siblinghood bringing out empathic and mature behaviors in firstborns, such as offering a pacifier to a baby in need of comfort, or a toy to one in need of stimulation. Offers of help and affection from an older sibling toward a younger one are soon followed by similar behaviors by a younger child toward the older one. Friendly firstborn toddlers play with their newborn baby sisters and brothers by imitating them. This, in turn, soon leads to baby siblings reciprocating by copying their older siblings. In fact, studies show that siblings who engaged in early imitation games later enjoyed friendlier and more affectionate relationships.

What fuels early friendship between siblings? Less is known about sibling friendship than peer friendship. With the same peculiar one-sidedness leading to scientists overlooking jealousy between peers, studies for a long time ignored friendship between siblings. And so when researchers wanted to learn about early friendship, they studied peer interaction. When they wanted to learn about rivalry, they studied sibling interaction. Of course, rivalry is not limited to siblings, and friendship is not limited to peers.

Newer studies have attempted to find common ground between sibling and peer friendships, but such comparisons have been complicated by the fact that peer friendships involve children of the same age, while sibling friendships involve children of different ages. In any case, some evidence suggests that there are commonalities between sibling and peer friendships. These studies show that sibling friendships blossom under conditions much like those that inspire peer friendships. And again, the success of the relationship rides on whether children have something in common. Shared activity levels, common interests, and mutual enjoyment in a variety of play activities generate sibling warmth and companionship. The parallels between sibling and peer relationships work both ways. Positive relationships with siblings mirror positive relationships with peers, and conversely, a child's aggression toward siblings foretells aggression toward peers.

Common interests serve relationships in two significant ways: they foster companionship, and they counteract rivalry. The strength of a sibling relationship depends on whether satisfaction from companionship outweighs that from competition. As the importance of companionship goes up, the importance of rivalry goes down. And so, whether there is warmth or animosity between a pair of siblings depends on whether their relationship is important enough to withstand rivalry. Chances are, the closer two siblings are in age, the closer their interests, hence, the greater the probability that their friendship will offer enough companionship and be of sufficient value to hold rivalry in check. On the other hand, the loss of a widely spaced sibling's less satisfying company may not be much of a loss, leaving nothing to stand in the way of jealousy. For example, two siblings who know that they really need each other in order to continue a game of pitch and catch are two children who are motivated to resolve their disputes on their own. Simply put, companionship neutralizes jealousy.

Some research showed links between close spacing and children's poorer intellectual development. This work, however, was conducted some decades ago, at a time when young children obtained less stimulation from fathers and through preschool education. It was also more likely to be found true of children in large families where other known risk factors, such as crowding and poverty, negatively impact on children. Other early studies showed that a new baby's arrival triggers more fussing in two-year-olds than four-year-olds. Maybe so. But what exactly does this mean? It probably does not mean that two-year-olds feel more jealousy than four-year-olds, but rather, that a two-year-old, being younger than a four-year-old, will object more vigorously and openly to *anything*. Without much vocabulary, that is how a two-year-old expresses himself. Although early research documented younger children's greater fussing at the time of a sibling's arrival, the significance of their greater fussing has never been upheld through follow-up studies showing that the long-term outcomes are worse for closely spaced siblings. Future research may one day tell us whether two-year-olds really *feel* greater jealousy than four-year-olds. My hunch is that eventual insights into the origins of jealousy will someday reveal that two-year-old firstborns feel *less* jealousy than four-year-old firstborns. After all, having enjoyed half as many years of exclusive parental attention, they develop lesser expectations of receiving preferential treatment from parents.

Will close-in-age siblings have more fights? Perhaps. For siblings and peers alike, friendship comes as a package, and rivalry is part of the deal. But with closely spaced siblings, the fights will be less bitter, and they will go hand-in-hand with more contact, more companionship, and more fun. As a growing body of literature has begun to show, mild forms of sibling conflict can actually help children by giving them chances to learn how to roll with the punches, to negotiate, and to develop a sense of humor and an identity along the way. Eliminating sibling conflict through wide spacing comes at a high cost. The only way to be assured of no fights is to have no friends. Widely spaced siblings may have fewer fights, but then so do complete strangers.

A final point to keep in mind is this. If children get to choose their friends, they pick out children much like themselves. Active children choose active buddies, quiet children choose quiet buddies, and most children choose friends who are about their own age. If your firstborn child had a say in choosing his younger sibling, would he opt for a playmate, about his own age, or for a protégé, five years younger than himself, whom he could mentor? Most likely, he would opt for the playmate over the student, and the subsequent relationship would hold up for the very same reason that peer friendships hold up—good companionship is deeply satisfying. At present, we parents still do not have the option of determining whether a next-born child will be active or quiet, male or female. But we at least have some control over the child's age relative to that of his older sibling. Why not exercise this one option, and set the stage for what our children really want, and what we want for them, companionship?

Trade-Offs

In the short run, close spacing between births means that parents probably will have to deal with more fussing, and they certainly will have a more serious workload. But, as the years go by, the early advantages of spacing children for apart, such as sleep and peace and quiet, will decline, and the disadvantages will surface. Even as they get older, widely spaced children will not easily find companionship in each other. A five-year-old may have scant interest in a newborn baby, too young to be any kind of playmate. A six-year-old might find that playing "mommy" or "daddy" with a one-year-old can be fun, but for no more than fifteen minutes. A seven-year-old is mostly annoyed by a two-year-old who wants to chew on the crayons being used to draw a picture, or the blocks needed to build a structure. An eight-year-old can resent a three-year-old's inability to sit through the reading of a story. A nine-year-old can go nuts on a car trip with a four-year-old, who still cannot play a game of cards or checkers. A ten-year-old may feel that there is no point in asking parents for help with a homework assignment because the inevitable presence of a bored five-year-old is more of a headache than the help is worth. Preteens do not consider themselves in the same league as children, and teenagers feel well above preteens. In most places, children born four years apart will not be together during preschool, junior high, high school, or even college. And if they are of different genders, it is unlikely that widely spaced siblings will ever share the same hobbies, enjoy the same sports, play the same games, be on the same teams, participate in the same extracurricular activities, join the same clubs, have the same camp groupings, like the same friends, go to the same parties, or prefer the same sorts of entertainment during the entire period spent living under one roof.

As parents become aware of the differing tastes and needs of their widely spaced children they become increasingly responsive to them. And, instead of being energized and united by recreational activities, families end up drained and splintered. All too soon, parents discover that there is no way to satisfy both children, all at the same time, and before long, parents find themselves driven in opposite directions, each with only one child. Mom stays home with the two-year-old who needs a nap, while Dad takes the six-year-old to a movie. Mom takes a three-year-old to story time at the library, while Dad takes the seven-year-old to soccer practice. Mom does the violin lesson with the four-year-old, while Dad helps the eight-year-old with a science project. As extracurricular activities snowball into ever more time-consuming events, parents find that one child's important game can overlap with another child's recital, and neither parent is able to attend both events. To make things worse, more often than not, the division of labor between parents is set along gender lines. Fathers do the sports, science, and outdoor events; mothers do the art, literary, and indoor activities. Finally, simply scheduling a meal, with everyone seated together at the dinner table, becomes unattainable. Even events as ordinary as watching television will not consist of two children, seated together in the den, chortling over a favorite sitcom and a shared bowl of popcorn. More likely, each child will have a television set in his own room, where he can watch the show of his choice privately, behind closed doors, undisturbed by anyone, including parents. Thus, wide age spacing divides not just siblings but whole families as well.

The strain on families is even greater if both parents are employed outside the home. Instead of positioning themselves for access to possible job promotions, parents of young children often opt for the "mommy," or "daddy" track, where the prospects of advancement are nil. These parents might choose to take only part-time work, or a position that does not include much travel, or a less responsible position that does not require going home with an overstuffed briefcase every evening. However, devoting more energy to parenting and less to a career entails a career sacrifice. The longer one stays on the parent track, the lower the chances of later reclaiming one's career. In fact, stay on the track too long, and you never get off.

If a parent is committed to wide age spacing *and* to devoting time to the children during their infancies, then she is stuck with a tough choice. She can either have a second child four or five years after the first and give up her career, having dedicated too many years to parenting, or she can save her career, but give up the second child. The feasibility of having a second child is further challenged by wide spacing in cases where women have delayed the birth of a first child. Waiting four years before having another child may not be an option for a mother who is reaching the end of her child-bearing years. Tragically, parents may feel cornered into making great sacrifices, which are often unnecessary. A parent can be dedicated to one child exclusively, or to two children nonexclusively. The latter option (close spacing) can lead to a substantial payoff: having both a career *and* a family with two children.

Having a second child, and a closely spaced second child, in particular, has added potential for unifying families. It contributes favorably to the roles fathers play in family life. The family with only one child is triadic. And under any circumstances, triangular relationships are fertile ground for rivalry. When children vie for parental attention, the result is sibling rivalry. On the other hand, when parents vie for children's attention, it sets the stage for yet another source of competition, known as gatekeeping. These are husband-wife conflicts over children's love, and more often than not mothers' stronger hold on this family treasure. Wives blame their husbands for intentionally choosing to be remote. Husbands blame their wives for keeping them at bay, driving them off instead of coaxing them in, while hogging up all of the baby's love and affection for themselves. A recent characterization of fathers as "also-rans" is an implicit illustration of one father's recognizing that spouses are in competition against one another. The deprecating term also implies that in the race for stature in their children's eyes, fathers often feel they come in second.

As long as parents outnumber children, potential for gatekeeping conflicts are rife. Moreover, the longer parents put off having a second child, the greater the chances that such conflicts will escalate, or even become permanently unresolved. Waiting for the mother-infant relationship to solidify before having a second child is a good idea, but once the mother-infant bond is secure, waiting longer does not make the relationship more secure. Instead, the bond can become too solidified, in a sense, cemented to the point where it is impenetrable by fathers. A danger of wide spacing is that it keeps fathers out of the loop for too long.

Even worse, *very* wide spacing, in effect, creates a family with two "only" children. Instead of rapidly doing away with the unstable mother-father-infant triangle through the quick addition of a second child, the late addition of a very widely spaced second child simply sets up yet another triangle. And as wives, for a second time, hold the upper hand because of their earlier and greater contact with infants, husbands may again fail to compete successfully for access to their children's affection and may find themselves the odd man out of *both* triangles. This sorry situation is avoidable. With close spacing between births, family unification occurs sooner, before the cement of the mother-infant bond hardens. The sooner fathers get involved, the better their chances of integrating themselves into the mother-infant bond, and the less likely that they will be locked out, possibly for a second time, and possibly for good.

Oddly, the early hardship of caring for two young children has a silver lining; it can help take fathers out of the periphery and draw them into the action. Rearing a one-year-old toddler while pregnant with a second child, and later parenting both a newborn baby and a two-year-old toddler, are demanding tasks. In fact, these tasks are so formidable that even the most possessive mother would have to loosen up some control over the children, and even the most alienated and reluctant father would have to feel impelled to somehow weave himself into the fabric of family life. It is difficult to imagine how gatekeeping can be an issue when a family has closely spaced children.

Gatekeeping is even less likely to become problematic if a third child joins the family before too long. Indeed, there may even be some truth in the frequently noted observation that there is *less* jealousy among siblings in large families. This is a peculiar sort of observation. One would think that when the number of children increases, the chance of any one child accessing parental attention becomes slimmer, thereby stepping up competitiveness among sisters and brothers. How could diminished access to such a vital resource as parental attention defuse sibling rivalry? One possible explanation for this counterintuitive observation is that as the number of children goes up, rivalry between husbands and wives for access to children goes down.

Perhaps when there are plenty of children to go round, opportunities for gatekeeping conflicts are diminished, and parents become less competitive with each other. And as parents become less competitive, they become more cooperative, as do their children, resulting in less sibling rivalry. Sometimes parents of closely spaced children can find *themselves* in a relationship that is friendlier and more intimate just because they are forced into cooperating with each other, and because exclusiveness has been restored to the marital relationship. Ultimately, the best way to ensure a man's interest in his children is to ensure his interest in the marriage. And one way of ensuring interest in the marriage is by minimizing gatekeeping conflicts.

These days, nuclear families are getting smaller and smaller, while members of the extended family are living farther and farther apart. Without large families and troops of relatives close by, our children do not have bunches of siblings and cousins with whom to grow up. At the same time, most of our marriages and careers are strained enough without the added divisiveness of being sent in opposite directions by children in search of companionship unavailable at home. Nor do we need unnerving byproducts of wide spacing, such as gatekeeping issues, pulling us apart from our spouses and children. More than ever, siblings need each other for companionship, and spouses need every ounce of help in keeping their families, their careers, and their marriages together. If there is an antidote for sibling rivalry, it is friendship between children themselves. And the bond that links children can also help bind families. If close spacing comes with a cost, it is not to children's emotional development but to parents facing the enormous burden of child rearing during the first year or two. In the long run, however, close spacing may mean closer siblings and closer families.

Summary

Wide spacing between births has been recommended on the assumption that firstborns gain from exclusive parental attention and through formal methods of preparation. Research, however, shows no evidence that toddlers are advantaged by either of these mechanisms. Nor is there evidence that they benefit from wide spacing. To the contrary, it is possible that wide spacing may actually leave families shortchanged.

In the long run, wide spacing between siblings discourages friendship, and, in turn, unleashes rivalry. Large age differences also promote divisiveness between parents by compelling them to respond separately to their widely spaced children's incompatible social and intellectual needs. Further, by necessitating choices between sacrificing either the second income or the second child, wide spacing is unrealistic for dual-career couples. Finally, wide spacing prolongs the existence of an inherently unstable set of triangular relationships in which adults outnumber children. In this kind of triadic milieu, paternal involvement is evoked later, sometimes too late for it to matter at all.

Chapter Eight

Preventing Sibling Rivalry

> How do I love thee?
> Let me count the ways.
>
> —Elizabeth Barrett Browning,
> *Sonnets from the Portuguese*

STRATEGY FIVE in preventing sibling rivalry consists of preparing an infant for the loss of exclusiveness by building a bedrock of love and love skills. What are these skills? How do they work?

The maxim "An ounce of prevention is worth a pound of cure" applies to many of life's challenges, including success in managing sibling rivalry. Thus, preventive measures are not merely the first steps toward managing sibling rivalry, they are also the best steps. A young child's adjustment to the arrival of a sibling depends on her early emotional development, in general, and on the emergence of love and jealousy, in particular. Since these evolve during the first year of life, the most effective preventive measures are those undertaken during this early, sensitive period. So, do not wait until your firstborn can talk. Do not wait until a second-born infant arrives, or is even on the way. The best time to start preparing for a sibling's arrival is when you bring home your *first* child, not the second.

Parents can take one of two approaches during this early period of emotional development. These methods are not equal.

The first provides an infant with experiences that discourage
expectations of receiving exclusive or preferential attention.
Although there are limits to what psychologists have learned
about infant development, they are clear on this: babies develop
best when they are cared for lovingly. Loving care involves
attending to infants' basic needs for food, safety, shelter, and
cleanliness. It also involves providing them with stimulation
through affection and play. Infants thrive most successfully when
their needs are met by attention that is offered promptly and in
abundance.

Limiting jealousy by limiting the quality of parental attention
to infants has some serious consequences. This point is sharply
illustrated by findings of research on jealousy in infants of
depressed mothers. Denied special attention from their emotionally restricted mothers, my colleagues and I discovered infants of

depressed mothers develop less jealousy. Unfortunately, as Lynne Murray and Peter Cooper at the University of Reading point out, these infants show a whole range of physical, social, emotional, and cognitive deficits. Moreover, the outcomes of postpartum depression are not merely transitory; the deleterious effects on children are enduring. What this tells us is that jealousy can be reduced by limiting parental attention, but at a huge cost. As infants' jealousy is diminished, so is love and every other aspect of healthy development.

Study after study shows that infants are less prone to fussiness, crying, and illness, and more inclined to enjoy good health, secure relationships, and positive emotional development if they receive prompt and sensitive attention. Most assuredly, it would be impossible to give an infant this high level of attention without also giving her the feeling of being special. The possibility that an infant would *not* feel like the number one baby when her needs are, in fact, the number one priority in the household, is unrealistic. Is it possible to nurture an infant's healthy development without also cultivating jealousy? The answer is no, so a healthy first step in preventing sibling rivalry requires an entirely different approach.

The Love Vocabulary

A toddler's adjustment to the arrival of a sibling is based on his innate temperament, and while it is true that biologically based temperament itself cannot be changed, much can be done about the way in which it eventually unfolds into personality. This process of unfolding begins with an infant's command of social skills, or a "love vocabulary." Managing this developmental process is the key to preparing an infant for the loss of exclusiveness entailed by a sibling's arrival. And so, early in infancy, what counts most is how an infant is taught to express and elicit love, not jealousy.

Remarkably, children express love, and they evoke our love, by being powerful communicators of emotion at very early stages of development. Long before they have any use of language, infants reach us and bind us to them through their brilliant command of this wordless code, which includes "positive love signals" as well as "negative love signals."

Positive Love Signals

To behold a child's love is to have a gift so precious, few can resist. If we choose to become parents, we do so largely for the sheer pleasure of being cherished by our children. And infants display behaviors that are essential to communicating love from the moment they are born. They start by showing interest. Although the visual capabilities of newborn infants are limited, they can focus their eyes on nearby objects, and they can turn their heads. Even if an infant is too delicate to show these clear signs of attentiveness, he will show subtle signs of paying attention. Watch a newborn infant closely and you will see his breathing slow down and become rhythmic and his body become utterly still as he concentrates all his energies on sensing an event. Regardless of whether an infant can turn his head and look around, or just concentrate quietly, he does so selectively. Infants focus on events that are of interest to them. And interesting events are those that bring pleasure. Among the most interesting sources of stimulation are social stimuli. Within moments of delivery, infants take pleasure in the sound of their mothers' voices and the sight of adults' faces.

Infants' interests in social stimulation can also lead them to track a moving object. If an adult's face is close by and veers slowly from one side of the infant's face to the other, newborns will actually make eye contact and then accompany the moving face with their own eyes and heads. When parents talk softly to their infants, and especially if they use a slow, singsong voice, infants will be even more inclined to stay focused on a source of stimulation. Infants' interests are accompanied by their feelings of joy. Even premature infants, so delicate they can barely move their heads or even open their eyes, have been known to smile upon hearing the ebb and flow of an adult's lilting voice. Newborns can also imitate adults' facial expressions. If you smile at a newborn infant, the baby will sometimes smile back.

By the age of two to three months, an infant's interest in receiving social stimulation from any adult evolves into the ability to show signs of recognition. People are treated differently from objects. At this point, infants will spontaneously deploy their eye contact and visual tracking skills to seek out particular adults, and then smile brightly upon making contact. These social smiles suggest that infants recognize familiar individuals. At six months of age, infants can exhibit laughter. By now, babies laugh not merely when they're tickled but also because they're developing a sense of humor. Toward the end of the first year, infants demonstrate smiles that glisten with wide-eyed anticipation and eagerness and often with direct eye contact. Such smiles tend to be seen when an infant greets his mother or father after some period of separation. Because these smiles are usually reserved for specific individuals, they reflect more than mere recognition; they suggest strong preferences for selected persons.

Intimacy is also communicated through physical contacts. Shortly after birth, infants can mold themselves in an adult's arms, as if cuddling up, and in a manner that clearly suggests that they are being comforted. They can grasp hold of a source of support, sometimes with enough strength in their fingers to actually support themselves by clinging onto an adult's clothing. Infants are soothed by being touched, relaxed by massage, and eased by the sound of a soft voice. They are comforted by being held, and their best sleep is in bed with parents. Crawlers follow their mothers and fathers. Beginning walkers stumble along while holding onto adults' skirts and shins. They reach toward adults to avoid toppling over and feeling fearful. Infants' holding and cuddling evolve into hugs and kisses. By the age of one year, these signs of affection are no longer given out gratuitously. They are reserved for preferred individuals, usually parents.

Eye contact, visual tracking, smiling, cuddling, holding, following, hugging, and kissing are positive love signals. These attractive behaviors communicate love and affection and act as bonding agents by drawing adults to infants. They evolve sequentially, in a pattern marked by growing complexity. Thus, they start off as simple signals, based on an infant's general interest in eliciting social stimulation, and they evolve into well-organized patterns of more elaborate behaviors. They also grow through a gradual process of social refinement. Whereas early signals are directed toward *any* adult who shows a desirable pattern of stimulation, later signals become reserved for recognized persons, and are then targeted toward highly preferred individuals.

Negative Love Signals

Love can be expressed through negative love signals as well. This oxymoron refers to reactions that come across as frankly unappealing behaviors, at least on the surface. On some deeper level, however, they signify the presence of love. Thinking of them as "unsociable social skills" might be one way of making sense of these intriguing behaviors that emerge early in infancy.

By three months of age, infants expect to enjoy their parents' smiling faces and cheerful voices. But just as infants take pleasure in social stimulation, they take *dis*pleasure in a lack of it. Ed

Tronick and his colleagues at Harvard University School of Medicine found that when mothers adopt an expressionless, still face, their infants get upset. Yet, sadly, some infants show no concern over their mothers' dead expressions. As Tiffany Field discovered, babies who are accustomed to receiving care from depressed and despondent mothers are unperturbed by a parent's emotional neglect. Thus, well-cared-for infants' fussing and whining in response to an adult's emotional absence is a way of saying, "Don't ignore me." Even though this appeal for emotional engagement does not constitute an attractive display of behavior, it engages adults' emotional attention and involvement. And, in the process, it binds adults to infants.

By one year, infants show separation distress when their parents are physically absent. Infants will protest a parent's departure by showing sadness, as if to say, "Don't leave me." Prolonged separations will produce profound sadness, and a parent's failure to return can precipitate extreme grief and depression in infants, as was documented in early studies on children who were orphaned during infancy. Separation distress occurs only in circumstances that involve certain individuals in particular. Infants miss only those whom they love. Thus, this demand for involvement is again, if not a pretty way, certainly an effective way, of binding adults to infants. But not just any adults, only beloved adults.

The final negative love signal is jealousy protest. By their first birthday, infants want emotional and physical involvement with adults, and they want it all to themselves, exclusively. With the ability to expect exclusive attention comes the ability to feel distress in situations where exclusive attention is denied. An infant's protest is a way of saying, "Don't be unfaithful." Whereas infants are unperturbed by having to share the attention of a stranger, they can be infuriated by having to share the attention of parents and other nurturing caregivers. As with other negative love signals, jealousy protests are not very appealing, but they succeed in getting the adults' attention and involving them with their infants. And again, they engage only those adults whom the infant loves.

Blessings and Mixed Blessings

Adults are enthralled when they observe the keen interest and sizable effort put forth by a newborn infant as he struggles to make contact with them. Parents are proud and awed that their infants want to see them and touch them. Mothers are delighted that their infants can recognize their voices, and we are all moved by an infant being calmed by our touch. Knowing that we are a source of pleasure to an infant is heartening, even inspiring. Studies demonstrate that early parent-infant experiences, in which infants' amazing capabilities are demonstrated for parents, foretell positive outcomes for infants and the parent-child relationship. By merely being shown that their infants need them and respond to them, parents become so touched that they put out extra effort to engage their infants and foster their development. When infants eventually exihibit social smiles, parents become even more ecstatic. To be the object of an infant's smile is perhaps the greatest compliment anyone can receive. The pleasure of being bestowed with an infant's happy gaze is often recorded in memory as one of life's crowning achievements.

If positive love signals are a blessing, then negative love signals are a mixed blessing. When infants demonstrate separation distress, these woeful events are not considered peak moments in our lives. Parents don't boast about it; they lament it. Nor are there benefits from having this feature of an infant's behavior drawn to a parent's attention. Highlighting it would forecast parental anguish and embarrassment, not pride. We do not nurture fond memories of these outbursts; we try to forget them.

Jealousy protests are commemorated with similarly pallid levels of enthusiasm. No one needs to have sibling rivalry brought to their attention. Parents are usually all too aware of it, as well as their own shortcomings in dealing with the problem. Those who have lived through raising highly competitive children do not feel uplifted by reliving the memory. They feel pain.

Seen in this grim light, it might be difficult to appreciate why negative love signals, if so deplorable, could be considered even a mixed blessing. The fact is that positive love signals have a drawback; they are not absolutely selective. Radiant smiles, which parents live for, are not always reserved for Mommy and Daddy. So far, psychologists are unaware of any particular sort of smile known to be reserved uniquely for parents, 100 percent of the time. As a parent, I have to admit that it saddens me to report that the most brilliant smiles that we parents receive are shared with Micky Mouse, Big Bird, even Ronald McDonald. One of the most memorable smiles that I can personally recall was evoked in my three-year-old daughter, Natalie, when she was informed that we had tickets to see the play *Peter Pan* and that she would get to see Tinker Bell. The thought of the magical fairy, flying out on stage, elicited a radiant smile and wide-eyed excitement that was rarely, if ever, matched during her entire childhood. Physical contacts are not much better. Strong embraces, with clenched fists and eyes squeezed shut are usually reserved for family members. Regrettably, however, the very same hugs are also enjoyed by the family pet, a newly acquired teddy bear, and Santa Claus.

Contrasting with positive love signals, negative love signals are expressed more selectively, uniquely reserved for attachment figures, such as devoted family members and caregivers. So, while it true that my daughter might have given Tinker Bell her best smile, it is also true that she showed no sign of falling apart when the dear fairy departed. Nor was Natalie even slightly devastated upon discovering that when Tinker Bell waved at her, the fairy also waved at everyone else in the audience. Yet if *I* had left Natalie, even for a moment, or given her no more attention than any other child in the audience, she would have exploded. When adults lament that children reserve their worst behavior for their parents, they are not lying.

Psychologists interested in measuring the quality of parent-infant relationships do not measure infants' positive love signals. No special, all-telling twinkle, smile, or hug permits researchers the "Aha!" response. Until scientists identify a unique gesture, kiss, or embrace that is strictly reserved for parents, the best we can do is examine how infants act when their parents are emotionally or physically absent, or are focused on another child. And so, we measure negative love signals. If an infant fails to show any sign of distress when his mother shows a still face, vanishes unexpectedly, or attends kindly to another child, we are alerted to the possibility that this could be a troubled relationship.

When their infants communicate, "Don't ignore me," "Don't leave me," and "Don't be unfaithful," parents are aware, on some level, that these appeals are meant only for them. And because these demands are made solely of parents, and never of Mickey Mouse, Big Bird, Ronald McDonald, Santa Claus, or Tinker Bell, they are extremely compelling. In fact, they are so powerful, that even though they are not the "nicest" love signals, they actually work the best.

Negative love signals have a second advantage over positive love signals. In addition to being more selectively given out, they are noisier. Quite literally, infants make a racket when they protest their parents' departing or paying attention to another child. As a result, it is less likely that a negative love signal will go unnoticed, and once it has come to the parents' attention, it can be difficult to ignore.

The Balance

By having access to a highly developed vocabulary of love signals, infants are supplied with skills vital for obtaining what is most precious to them at a time of transition, parental love and attention. By having command of *positive* signals, infants have the option of enlisting emotional support through use of attractive behaviors. Children who can draw on these social skills are able to handle emotional challenges with grace.

Who are these socially adept infants? They are the ones who look toward their parents knowing that their bright gaze will engender sparkling eye contact in return. Infants who smile at their parents are infants who know that their smiles will elicit warm smiles in turn. Similarly, infants who laugh, coo, play, and snuggle up to parents are those who know that their parents will reciprocate with playful chatter and warm affection. Infants develop rich vocabularies of positive love signals. Some prefer smiles and eye-contact games, such as peek-a-boo. Others love games with turn taking, or playful roughhousing, or gentle teasing. It can be the sound of your voice, singing and music, or cuddling that makes an infant thrive. Socially adept infants know what works for them. And if they are fortunate in having several loving caregivers, they even know each caregiver's specialty and will tailor their appeals accordingly, so that particular types of attention will be sought out and promoted in particular caregivers.

This key to accessing parental attention is helpful in all sorts of stressful situations as well as social situations. The arrival of a sibling is not the only stressful situation that an infant will encounter, and mothers and fathers will not be the only ones whose attention is sought out by infants. An infant who can use eye contact, cooing, smiling, and affection in order to get attention will be seen as a charming baby, as irresistible to parents as to siblings, peers, relatives, and child care workers. The infant whose positive pleas for attention are heard when a sibling arrives is the infant whose pleas are heard when other adversities are at hand as well.

Without access to a vocabulary of positive love signals, infants simply resort to using negative love signals like jealousy protests and crying for attention. These noisy and emotionally compelling signals are readily noticed and easily read by adults, so they tend to get results, even from parents who fail to notice or read their infants' more subtle positive signs. The fussing, whining, and crankiness seen in young infants who have been neglected are the result of never having acquired or developed more positive ways of attracting attention. When such behavior becomes the sole means of eliciting parental attention, negative love signals are almost impossible to eradicate.

Even sadder are the unfortunate cases where infants seem to have no "vocabulary" at all. Those who have suffered severe emotional deprivation will show neither positive signals nor negative signals. Having determined that nothing they do can successfully gain attention, these lost babies exert no communicative efforts whatsoever. They do not smile or bother looking toward adults. Even crying seems a waste of energy to these poor babies.

Preparing Toddlers for a Sibling's Arrival

A child's adjustment to a sibling can take a little while, and there may be dips along the way. How long it takes, and how smoothly it progresses, depends largely on the extent to which a firstborn has positive love signals at his disposal. Some infants are more familiar and successful with positive signals, and so they are less inclined toward using negative signals. By contrast, other infants are more accustomed to success with negative signals, so they develop less reliance on positive signals. Past experience and habitual use of a love vocabulary establishes a response style that sets the stage for the reaction to a newborn sibling's arrival.

In times of stress, an infant's skill in eliciting parental attention is more than just a way of enlisting an adult in a playful game of communication. It serves as a coping mechanism. Faced with a let-down, adults also will draw on various personal resources. Optimally, these resources already exist in our lives. If we take comfort from calling up a friend for support and advice, it helps if we already have an established friendship. If we are perked up by a game of tennis, we need to know how the sport is played. In a real crisis, we might draw on a number of resources to help us cope. Just knowing that those resources exist helps us get through hard times.

Infants and children also need coping mechanisms, which they find hard to acquire under duress. The arrival of a sibling is hardly the ideal time to start acquiring positive love signals. Imagine being thrown into the English Channel and asked to swim to the opposite shore when you are basically a nonswimmer. Or think of how receptive you would be to the prospect of performing an exercise in advanced calculus when you can barely pass a test in simple arithmetic. Belated efforts fail, especially when undertaken under stressful conditions. Under such circumstances, learning a skill that might otherwise be manageable appears insurmountable. Someone who is drowning wants a life raft, not swimming lessons. Anyone about to fail a calculus exam wants to cheat, not get a math tutor. Under pressure, we take shortcuts. So do infants.

Unfortunately, parents often don't start thinking about instilling positive love signals until their firstborn children bitterly face the arrival of a baby sibling. Yet, this is not an ideal time to start to teach a child "how to behave." If a child is accustomed to getting parental attention largely through whining, crying, and temper tantrums, she is bound to have difficulty learning more positive strategies just when taxed by the emotional burden of having to adjust to a newborn sibling.

Young children who have developed a strong reliance on negative signals for engaging adults' attention can actually become more adept at them when a new baby appears on the scene, and negative behaviors often escalate. That's when beleaguered parents—overwhelmed by their children's ugly behavior—start looking for professional help from community parenting classes, pediatricians, and therapists. With help, parents can work on developing more positive behaviors in their infants. Although the task is by no means impossible, it is certainly made more difficult by the delayed timing.

Even when toddlers have an established pattern of using positive signals, the immediate response to a newborn's arrival will include some negative signals. Negative styles for demanding attention and exclusiveness are hardly unknown, even in infants who have a sparkling command of positive behaviors. Hot-tempered infants, in particular, no matter how socially skillful, will show some jealousy. At this point, much depends on how parents react to their firstborns' jealousy. Because a toddler will require parental support when a newborn sibling arrives, giving him command of a positive love vocabulary for eliciting support is necessary to success in coping with jealousy, but this alone is not enough.

Preparing *Parents* for the Sibling's Arrival

When a newborn sibling arrives, some parents make the mistake of yielding to their firstborns' every demand, including their negative ones. Parents might feel that their firstborn children are emotionally fragile, so "denying" attention could have disastrous consequences for the child. Or, parents might regard a sign of jealousy as a sign of serious mental disturbance. Alternatively, parents

Preventing Sibling Rivalry
Strategy Five

Sibling bonds are built on the love between firstborns and their parents, and that love shows up through an infant's positive love vocabulary: the wordless code of social skills, emotion cues, and attractive behaviors that serve as coping mechanisms by helping infants elicit parental love and support during times of stress.

Nurture a strong command of this code in your infant during her first year of life and then trust in its strength when a newborn comes along. Show optimism, be generous with praise and encouragement, and be stable in providing support. Finally, resist the temptation to succumb to jealousy's powerful positive message; believe in your child's love for you, and he, in turn, will rise to the occasion with grace.

may perceive the loss of exclusiveness as such a stressful event that any kind of behavior in a firstborn child is warranted. Finally, they might simply feel so flattered by their toddler's jealousy that their hearts melt, and they cave in. These are all concerns that need some serious rethinking.

Have Faith

Imagine a parent's difficulty as he observes his child teeter while learning how to walk, or gulp mouthfuls of pool water while learning how to swim, or fumble while learning how to hang upside down on the playground monkey bars. Children learn how to ride bicycles, sometimes with no hands on the handlebars, to zig-zag their way on roller blades, and to skateboard downhill, barely in control. As we parents watch, we try *not* to look petrified. We mask our fear and look on with confidence. So when a child puts his head underwater, we try not to hold our breaths, and when he crashes into a linebacker, we try not to wince. No matter how much we love our children, we recognize that we cannot do everything for them. Instead, we believe in their fortitude. We stand back. Patiently, we await success and show our support by cheering them on in the spirit of, "You can do it!"

Now think of a different scenario. Imagine a child perched at the end of a diving board, with his nose pinched shut and his cheeks bursting with air. When he turns to his parents, they do *not* mask their fear. Instead, they gape at their precariously balanced child with horror in their eyes. Rather than saying, "You can do it," they are saying, "You *cannot* do it. You're too weak. It's too hard, We do *not* believe in you." Of course, the child's spirit is broken and, in turn, he does not jump. If this child happens to be particularly timid by nature, he may, in fact, never jump. Unlike some of his bolder and more reckless peers, he might simply pack it in for good and never again try to overcome his fear of diving.

Emotional hurdles are not terribly different. Adjusting to a sibling is an emotional challenge, one that a child faces largely on his own. Parents can only help. They do so by providing their children with a foundation of social skills and emotional strength, and by then believing in them. This requires recognizing whether a firstborn is capable of expressing love and eliciting loving attention through use of positive signals. Does this child make eye contact with you? Does he smile at you? Does he show affection? Is this a happy, playful child? If the answer is yes, then have faith in the child's psychological fortitude to meet the challenge. Mask your fear, stand back a little, be patient, and expect success. Let your child succeed through his own emotional resources.

Show Optimism

Like any good coach, set an example. Sometimes parents come home with a baby sister or brother, cringing with dread and consumed with guilt, as if they were about to deliver a blow, not a baby. Firstborns pick up on the mood set by their parents and mirror it. If parents cower with fear or anguish, firstborns will act as though they had been wounded and are entitled to compensation. The arrival of a second child is not a tragedy, even to a child who might not fully understand. In fact, it is often the case that parents will show joy in situations where children do not immediately comprehend the source of it. High-spirited parents bring home new flavors of ice cream, bicycles children cannot ride, and books on topics children know nothing about. When these objects are not happily received by children, parents are sympathetic, but they do not express regret. Rather, they persist in the belief that their own good spirits will soon be matched by those of their children. Usually they are right. As research repeatedly shows, parents are powerful role models. Happiness is catchy, and especially at times when children are more inclined than ever to look toward parents for emotional guidance. Act as though congratulations, not condolences, are in order, and a firstborn will eventually come around.

If parents feel that adapting to a sibling is beyond their firstborn's psychological capacity, their lack of confidence will be transmitted, and their most dreaded expectations will turn into grim reality. Time and again, research has shown that when parents believe that a child is weak and vulnerable, a child begins to act weak and vulnerable. Conversely, when parents believe in a child's strengths, those strengths flourish. Parental attitudes are an extraordinary phenomenon. Whether we are concerned with physical or emotional challenges, we encourage success through our upbeat attitudes, and we precipitate failure through our dismal forecasts.

> Rachel looked deeply into her daughter's face, panicked over the prospect of finding her own face, a tormented one she had had many years ago when presented with a baby brother. Allen's birth had been a nightmare for her but a dream come true for her father, who so much wanted a son and who made it clear that Rachel, being only a girl, had come as a disappointment. Whereas Rachel had to work hard, be perfect really, for the most meager sign of approval, in the years that followed, Allen had only to be present in the room for his father to light up with adoration and joy.
>
> But instead of witnessing her daughter's torment, two-year-old Melanie just stared blankly at the little bundle that was her baby brother, Jack. Then she turned to her mother with a quizzical look that said, "Now what?" Despite her instinct to sweep up her daughter and promise to protect her, Rachel just smiled at Melanie realizing, after all, that the searching expression on this brave little girl's face hardly qualified as the nightmare response she had so dreaded. Then Melanie brightened up and smiled too, first at Rachel, then at the baby.

Show Encouragement

When it comes to a child's adjustment to a sibling, a realistic notion of success depends on the individual child. If she reacts with anger, you applaud *any* grimace that is short of anger. If he is cautious, you cheer signs of approach—*any* signs of approach—regardless of the form they might take. A child might be willing to look at the newly arrived baby, or just be in the same room. If even that is out of the question, perhaps the child can draw a picture for the baby and have the "letter" delivered to the bassinet. A sign of progress may not be easily identified, but if you watch carefully, something heartening is bound to occur eventually, even if it happens only inadvertently. Sometimes children stop yelling only to come up for air. Even this constitutes a window of opportunity for raising a child's spirits with a strong show of parental support, encouragement, and confidence in her emotional strength.

When applied steadily, patiently, and for appropriate behaviors, parents' positive attitudes and encouragement will gradually win over a firstborn and defuse jealousy when a newborn arrives. When these efforts are successful, even minimally, go ahead and celebrate. Take pride in a child's effort and hard-won triumph. Do not act surprised by a child's accomplishments, nor trivialize the importance of small achievements. Remember that unlike the child on the diving board who was so discouraged by his parents' lack of confidence that he shied away from the board and gave up on diving forever, a jealous child does not have the option of shying from the pain brought on by jealousy.

Parents' identifying and encouraging their toddler's attractive behaviors will work particularly well if parents also downplay attention to their children's *un*attractive behavior. In research where young siblings' jealousy was ignored and their prosocial behaviors were praised, jealousy was effectively reduced. So stay focused on positive consequences. There's nothing wrong with prizes like toys, candy, and gifts, but the ones that work best are the things in life that count the most—a wink, a smile, a whispered word of praise, a kiss.

Show Stability

Some children, on the other hand, will react to a new sibling by showing the infant a smile or by offering her a toy or imitating her gurgling baby noises. These attractive behaviors are the "home runs" of child development. They deserve hearty and *continuous* applause. Sometimes parents and relatives make the mistake of paying attention to a firstborn only during the immediate period when the newborn arrives. When they observe a friendly reaction in this child, they deduce that the child is not jealous. Believing that jealousy is some sort of psychological defect, they sigh with relief in the newfound knowledge that their firstborn is not afflicted by it. Then, having dismissed the problem of jealousy, they abruptly withdraw support and proceed to simply ignore the child. Of course, their congratulations are premature. All too soon, the perfect little darling morphs into a raging monster, as parents bemoan "reality setting in."

During the last days of her third trimester, Magen dedicated all of her time and strength to her firstborn child, Jeremy. It was a bittersweet time, immense indulgence set against a looming sense of separation and loss over the upcoming conclusion to a four-year-long exclusive bond with her son, and some concern that Jeremy had inherited her weakness, a strong streak of jealousy. All too soon, Kelley was born and the peaceful hiatus ended abruptly.

The hoopla around Kelley's arrival was euphoric as dozens of friends and relatives came by, each bearing gifts for the baby and Jeremy as well, who, in his entire four years hadn't consumed the amount of candy packed away that one week. In the joyous commotion of people, gifts, and candy, Jeremy hadn't shown so much as a trace of jealousy. "What a lucky break," thought Magen. Feeling relief about the way Jeremy was behaving, once the excitement had died down, Magen was eager to finally turn all her attention to Kelley with the same full devotion she had once reserved for Jeremy. Then, seemingly out of nowhere, Jeremy exploded. He shrieked that when the relatives left they forgot to take Kelley with them.

In fact, this firstborn child *was* jealous when the newborn arrived. When his positive behaviors met with only short-lived favorable reactions from adults, he merely switched tactics and resorted to using negative behaviors instead. By overlooking a child's attractive behaviors, or by taking them lightly, parents can actually generate jealousy responses belatedly. Family members may need to experiment to find just the right balance of loving attention that is reasonable and workable. In some instances where there is a marked drop in fussing over a firstborn child, it can occur merely because family members overdid their efforts in the first place. Out of frantic concern over a firstborn's adjustment, parents sometimes lavish their firstborns with so much attention that it is simply impossible for them to keep it up. The result, again, is a belated eruption of jealousy.

Firstborns can be indulged in so many ways. Some take delight in our smiles and cheerfulness. Others adore our singing or just the sound of our happy chatter. Some revel in affection, playfulness, words of endearment, or words of praise. Use whatever works. Do not wait for something spectacular to take place before offering encouragement. And do not overlook the needs of well-behaved children. Remember, they can switch tactics in either direction. Negative reactions can be molded into positive reactions, and positive ones can be transformed into negative ones. As a result, jealousy can be trained down, but it can also be trained up.

Show Resolve

Sometimes parents find themselves oddly reluctant to take control of jealousy. When trying to downplay their reactions, they feel awkward, unsure whether to offer a firm response to the spoken message, "I hate my baby sister," or yield to the *un*spoken message,

"I love you, Mommy" or "I love you, Daddy." Why is it so hard to resist jealousy's positive message?

Jenny never knew what loneliness meant until her second pregnancy. Having had to give up her job in marketing because of cramps and fainting spells, and with her husband, John, away on business more than ever, she found herself home alone all winter long with her son, Michael. Fortunately, this cheerful three-year-old child was utterly delightful. No matter how cranky and abandoned Jenny felt, Michael's sweetness kept her afloat throughout the pregnancy.

Michael's easygoing nature had her completely unprepared for dealing with the temper tantrums and hysterics that followed Laurie's birth. Jenny knew it was important to be firm, but she had no idea how difficult it would be to bring herself to show firmness. She felt guilty for hurting him by bring home another baby. She also felt that she owed him something for keeping her spirits alive all winter. After all, he certainly hadn't abandoned her when she'd been down. No, he still loved her even though she was being unfaithful. Indeed, at the very bottom of her heart was the fear that if she took a firm stand, he would turn on her. Who will love me then? she fretted.

Jenny tried consoling, comforting, and giving Michael every minute she could spare, but instead of getting better he only got worse. Then one day, Michael walked up to Laurie and bit her on the nose. Jenny didn't snap, and she certainly didn't flare up out of control. Instead, she cooly decided that enough was enough. From that point on, Jenny made it clear that she would put up with none of her son's misbehavior. If he wanted comfort or affection, Jenny thought to herself, he could get it, but not with jealousy. Being quick and eager for his mother's love, Michael figured this out soon enough, and he returned to his former warmhearted self.

Like Jenny, many parents feel that denying parental love in return for a child's jealousy constitutes a rejection of the child's love, or the child himself. Rejecting a child's jealousy is harsh only if he has no other way of communicating love at his disposal. In the more typical cases we've looked at throughout this book, when their jealousy protests are met with cool responses, toddlers simply figure out the benefits of trying a different, and more optimal, tactic for procuring parental support. This takes some parental resolve. Just as infants must be prepared to find positive ways of *expressing* love, parents must be prepared to find positive ways of *accepting* love. Keep in mind that, as the saying goes, it takes two to tango; a child's jealous outbursts are of no use unless he has a receptive listening partner. If you don't want to be a partner in the jealousy dance, you don't have to be. But it is your responsibility to make that decision and to then make those wishes known to your child. On their own, children do not miraculously deduce that when a sibling arrives, an uncivilized love signal might not be such a good idea.

Will rejecting a child's love result in the child holding back love in return? If a child loves her parents she will continue to do so even if her parents have rejected her jealousy. Parents just need to feel confident that they are loved. This isn't always easy. A second child's arrival is a trying time, not just for firstborns, but for parents as well. Some parents, like Jenny, are themselves so insecure and desperate for love that brushing off a firstborn's jealousy takes some selflessness. Others are so embroiled in problems that they simply don't hear the more positive, but more subtle, signals their firstborns are expressing. Especially for overwhelmed parents who feel needy themselves, it can be hard to give up the gratification that can be so easily derived from being the object of jealousy.

In the end, however, it is what parents *do* that counts. Toddlers excel at reading parents' facial expressions and body language. Through these, parents can express what they want their infants to know, even if it does not quite match what parents may really feel inside. And so, in response to a firstborn's jealousy, parents are called upon to mask their fear, and their pleasure as well.

Summary

Sibling bonds are built on the love between firstborns and their parents. The strength of a toddler's love and his ability to elicit love from his parents are key to his adapting to a newborn's arrival. Parental love and support can be enlisted through a variety of techniques, some more attractive than others. Socially skilled infants have a strong vocabulary of positive love signals, such as eye contact, smiling, laughter, playfulness, and physical affection. These appealing behaviors are cultivated by parents, ideally within an infant's first year of life, and well before a second infant arrives. When faced with stress from the loss of exclusiveness, these behaviors serve as coping mechanisms, available to toddlers needy of support. At the time of a second child's arrival, parents can further encourage healthy coping styles by believing in their firstborn's emotional strength, modeling upbeat attitudes, supporting positive behavior, downplaying attention to jealousy, and confronting their own inner tendencies to yield to jealousy.

Preventive steps toward managing sibling rivalry actually have more to do with molding love than molding jealousy. If an infant has a rich command of well-honed skills in communicating love, he will not be crushed when his parents fail to indulge his jealousy. Instead, he will resort to more positive ways of engendering parental love and support, and jealousy will be abated.

Chapter Nine

How to Develop Sibling Bonds

Jealousy is always born with love, but does not always die
with it.

—La Rochefoucauld, *Maxims*

STRATEGY SIX in preventing sibling rivalry has two goals for
developing sibling relationships. The first aims to defuse jealousy;
the second aims to engender friendship.

Throughout the course of first-year development, jealousy
evolves side-by-side with love. Together, love and jealousy come
into existence primarily as reflections of relationships with parents. Prior to a sibling's arrival, parents can do much to set up sibling bonds by molding the emergence of their firstborns' love. But
when a sibling appears on the scene, it finally comes time to tackle
jealousy, itself. Once a child meets his new sibling, he steps from
one love triangle into another. How should parents manage those
steps? For starters, let's ask a seemingly silly question.

What Is Sibling Rivalry?

Regardless of the source of conflict, discord of any kind between
siblings is referred to as sibling rivalry. The fact that we use just

one broad term to describe sibling conflict implies there's only one solution. This notion is simplistic and as reasonable as concluding that all forms of marital conflict are alike in nature, and that there is only one kind of marital therapy. Further, the term *rivalry* tends to suggest that every fight between siblings is rooted in jealousy. Yet, contrary to what many believe, jealousy, in its strict sense, is *not* at the core of every sibling battle. Although the green-eyed monster is a nasty monster, arguably the nastiest, it certainly isn't the only one. In sibling relationships, as in other love relationships, antagonism is driven by a variety of different and sometimes confusing motives.

Struggles between young siblings are aroused by different feelings, they serve different purposes, and, most assuredly, they are resolved through parents' employing different kinds of resolution techniques. Choosing one and determining whether parental involvement is warranted, and what form it should take, will depend on an understanding of what motivates sibling conflict. Some causes are superficial, and some are deep. Sometimes a fight is instigated by a clearly defined issue in dispute; other times the real source of contention is buried under layers of defense. In fact, some fights hardly have anything to do with what children appear to be fighting over. It is natural, of course, for parents to react in accordance with the level of animosity, and it is easier to address more obvious causes. Big fights over tangible issues naturally get priority. But building friendship between siblings takes something more. Conflicts between children, like those between adults, are rarely resolved without recognizing their true causes and then addressing each one distinctively and strategically. Struggles between siblings fall into four major categories: jealousy, frustration, dominance, and entertainment.

Jealousy Fights

Jealousy fights are aroused by fears of losing love. A child strikes out when he feels threatened with the loss of parental love. He'll strike out at anyone or for anything; the target of an attack might be quite incidental. His target could be any sibling, and not necessarily the one who actually did anything to spark aggression. In these situations, a child's aggression can appear on the surface to be "irrational" in the sense that it seems to be a random act of unprovoked hostility or anger. Primarily, fights fueled by jealousy are reflections of discord between children and their parents, not between children and their siblings, and are aimed at reaffirming the parent-child relationship.

Among the different kinds of sibling conflicts, jealousy fights are the only instances in which there is a threat of losing parental affection. Hence, these fights constitute instances where some amount of parental warmth and reassurance is warranted. Still, shows of tenderness must be extended with extreme care. Rewarding a child's aggression toward a sibling with a show of parental love can make for a dangerous mix. This combination will easily lead a child to draw the logical conclusion that aggression toward a sibling leads to positive outcomes, namely parental attention.

Parents are often aware of the perils of making parental affection a consequence of sibling aggression. So, in addition to offering reassurances of love, some also express strong reproach. Others are so stumped, they simply do nothing. Most use both methods. All three approaches fail miserably. In cases where parents provide reassurances as well as reprimands, children are provided with mixed messages. For older children, mixed signals often consist of a combination of conflicting verbal messages, such as, "I don't like your behavior, but I still love you." Other times, parents might offer mixed signals via some combination of verbal and nonverbal behaviors. For example, parents might extend verbal forms of reproach, as in "I am angry with you for breaking your brother's toy truck," in conjunction with positive behavior, such as replacing the broken toy instead of having the young offender do it himself, perhaps by giving up one of his own toys or paying for the replacement with his allowance.

With toddlers and young children, mixed messages usually consist of parents offering one message verbally, and a second message nonverbally. Typically, the verbal message expresses reproach, while the nonverbal message expresses affection. In the contest between words and deeds, however, deeds dominate. Period. So if a parent says, "I am very angry," while giving his child a reassuring hug, the message conveyed by the hug will override the message conveyed by the words. Hence, what the child will learn is that aggression begets affection. This would be especially true with a very young child, who is quite expert at reading parents' facial expressions and body language, but only a beginner at understanding spoken language.

In addition to discovering that aggression pays off, the child will learn that words are meaningless. Faced with conflicting messages, a child can quickly conclude that words are a source of confusion and that paying attention to them is a silly waste of time, so linguistic information should simply be disregarded. This is a very unfortunate lesson for young children to learn, since words, especially emotion terms, are vital to civilized behavior. The importance of understanding the difference between "Mommy is mad," and "Mommy is happy," for example, is a key step toward acquiring the rules of appropriate social behavior.

Children acquire vocabulary by pairing up particular sounds or words with particular things or events. For instance, we would teach a child what *apple* means by showing him an apple. What a young child would deduce if his parents verbally express anger while showing affection has to be quite baffling. To this muddled child, the word *angry* might not mean anything foreboding. Emotion terms, such as *angry,* are not acquired as easily as terms for concrete objects, such as apples. By providing mixed messages, the process of acquiring parts of speech that connote emotion is seriously impeded. So much for civilized behavior.

In other instances, parents provide two signals, both verbal, with conflicting meanings, as in "I am angry, but I love you." For young children these messages are so confusing, they contain no discernable information. When verbal messages are contradictory and no other cues are provided, the net result is a child finding out that sibling aggression results in no negative consequences. For toddlers, this is the equivalent of parents opting to take no action at all, which amounts to tacit approval. This dangerous lesson is obviously not what parents wish to teach their feisty young children.

Jealousy fights are best resolved by parents providing both reassurances and reproach, *but not at the same time.* A child's aggressive behavior demands swift, consistent disapproval. Choose a level of disapproval that is reasonable, then express it using words, eye contact, facial expressions, tone of voice, gestures, and body language that are *all* unequivocally negative, otherwise the message will not get through. A harsh response is rarely necessary, perhaps only in instances where an infant has been physically harmed. Although a jealous child may feel threatened with losing parental love, this is not the time to mention that he is still adored. Reassurances come later.

Wait for the hostile child to settle down—it might be only shortly after a hostile exchange—then soften your tone of voice, make eye contact, and smile. Keep up with the positive cues until an opportunity to spend some time together arises, perhaps the next time the baby is taking a nap or is asleep for the night. Then use that time to express reassurances. Do something pleasurable: smile, talk, play, read, sing, dance, cuddle, roughhouse, massage, hold hands, take a walk, or eat something delicious together. Choose a comfortable and personal way to convey how much you love this child. Do whatever your child enjoys doing, and do whatever showcases how happy you are to be the parent of this child, using words that are compatible with your warm behavior. Even two-year-olds can understand clear, simple phrases, such as "I love you," "You are a great kid," and "I'm so happy you're mine."

When a parent wants to communicate two different messages to a young child, timing is of the utmost importance. Separating the two messages in time is key to getting through. By being firm when sibling aggression takes place, and by being affectionate when a child is behaving appropriately, both messages will come across distinctly. They will not be contradictory, and one message will not cancel out the other. One connection will link aggression toward a sibling with negative consequences, such as reprimands. The second connection will link friendly behavior toward a sibling with positive consequences, such as reassurances of love. Even a very young child is capable of making two distinct connections and will understand that hostile behavior is not acceptable, *and* that she is loved.

Frustration Fights

Frustration fights are motivated by inflated expectations and acquisitiveness, or simply greed. These fights have less to do with relationships and more to do with self-interest. The theme of these conflicts is, "I expect more." And young children will expect more of everything. They will want more tangibles, such as food and toys. They will also want more intangibles, such as privileges. In particular, young children will want more of things that they like. But sometimes they will expect to have things they do not even care about, understand, or need. They will expect more toys than their arms can hold, and more ice cream than they can eat. They will wish to stay up later than their bodies can hold up, to have more space than they know what to do with, and to go places they are not interested in visiting. Mostly, children have little idea of how much they really need of anything. And so they simply operate on the principle that it is better to have too much than too little. Unless, of course, they are taught otherwise, by someone kindly providing a few reasonable guidelines.

Given the option, young children will also expect the privilege of enjoying more attention than they need. Easily, they can want a level of attention that is not humanly possible for a parent to give. When parents dole out an amount and form of attention, they are often aware of the discrepancy between the level they can give and the level their children would like to receive. This notwithstanding, parents decide on a level, and whatever its amount and quality, this is the level that young children will come to expect. And so, just as children learn that there are limits to how much ice cream they can eat, how late they can stay up, and how much space they can take up, they also learn that there are limits to how much attention they can demand. Certainly it is fair for a toddler to expect unlimited love, but the privilege of access to unlimited attention is out of the question.

Once a child gets the notion that he is entitled to some amount of an object, experience, or privilege, being denied it will create frustration and anger and, in popular parlance, a spoiled brat. Unintentionally, parents are sometimes a little erratic when giving out objects or privileges. Feeling especially generous or energetic one day, a parent might decide to take everyone out for ice cream, or let a baby sleep in the parents' bed, or allow a two-year-old to stay up and watch television on daddy's lap until midnight. Of course, the child will automatically expect to receive the same level of treatment on the next day. And when denied, he'll become upset, and understandably so. This is not so much a child who is spoiled, as a child who is frustrated because of having been misled.

Parents can learn much about minimizing frustration from watching the way in which child care centers operate. In general, children are better behaved with caregivers than with parents. This is true for a number of reasons, one of which is the consistency with which nursery schools and child care centers run their days. Usually, a day's events are charted out in advance, and there are few departures from the routine. Events such as arrival, dismissal, lunch, snacks, nap, playground time, circle time, and story time, occur at prearranged and unvarying times. With the day's predictability comes calm and even-tempered children.

In the process of acquiring notions about what to expect from adults, children develop requirements pertaining to *absolute* amounts. They also develop notions about *relative* amounts. This means that when ice cream is doled out, a child might expect to receive one scoopful. Additionally, he might also expect to receive an amount that is greater than that which his baby brother receives. Similarly, he might expect his bedtime to be later, and his stories to be lengthier. Children are keenly aware of how much they receive compared with other individuals, such as siblings. Frustrations readily flare up when a child is offered some level of an object, experience, or privilege that is less than what he expects to receive. But even if the absolute amount is acceptable, he will still be upset because he is being offered less than expected *relative to a sibling*. Any change in the expected magnitude of discrepancy can set the older sibling off.

Other times, parents lead children to expect equal and identical amounts of things—an invitation for discontentment. No two scoops of ice cream are exactly alike, and no two children have identical appetites. Children's needs for parental attention are not always identical either. Just as children can expect to receive unlimited love, but not unlimited attention, they can expect to receive fair treatment, but not equal treatment. And, deciding what is fair is up to parents, not children. A young child, who sees no reason why chocolate ice cream is not the ideal breakfast food, will not readily appreciate why a parent might need to spend an entire week-end working on an older sibling's science fair project.

Frustration fights are minimized by keeping expectations in line with reality. This means that parents must provide an environment in which the absolute and relative amounts of attention and objects are as reasonable and fair as possible. Above all, treatment of siblings and discrepancies between siblings need to be kept as constant as possible. If treats are made available to siblings, try to offer them on a regular basis. If children become accustomed to getting one ice cream each, every night after dinner, try not to change the pattern. Children can learn to live with some disparities between siblings if parents keep the differences fair and to a minimum. The key issue is not only about how much to give

whom, but the regularity with which it is given. Stick with a reasonable level of discrepancy, and try not to make exceptions. If the
pattern is so predictable it appears cast in stone, frustration will
be kept to a minimum. After all, what point is there in fighting if
the outcome is a foregone conclusion?

Dominance Fights

Dominance fights are another form of sibling conflict. These are
driven by needs for establishing superiority and are a common
force behind sibling discord. Rather than aiming to reestablish the
parent-child relationship, the primary goal of these battles is to
establish an identity. In this instance, the parent-child relationship
is secondary, while the child-sibling relationship itself is at issue.
Dominance fights are marked by intense competition, as siblings
challenge each other in innumerable ways, while both children
work on figuring out who they are.

The standard theme of these struggles is: "I'm bigger, I'm taller,
I'm stronger, I'm cooler," which can also be expressed less cor-
dially as: "You're smaller, you're weaker, you're dumber, you're a
dork." This form of bickering can actually intensify with age, as
the need to establish an identity comes only later, with an emerging sense of having an identity. A sense of self begins to evolve in
the second year of life, and building an identity takes years. But
from its very start, the journey toward self-discovery is filled with
competition for status, often between siblings. They compete not
merely to impress each other, but to impress themselves, to find
out who they are. By winning, or establishing dominance, they
show themselves that they are competent. And budding identities
thrive on such knowledge.

Dominance fights erupt as siblings compete over issues that are
sometimes of substance, but more often they are trivial and incon-

sequential. These are squabbles for rights over some object, privilege, or status. In these situations, parents must address each child's need to build a healthy self-image. At the same time, however, they must also make it clear that when children wish to satisfy their needs to define themselves and develop their identities, such needs are to be met, but not at each other's expense.

Parents can learn much about fostering this kind of personal growth from team leaders, such as athletic coaches. Coaches prize competitiveness, but they are also well aware that a successful team will not be composed of individuals who hate each other. Effective coaches are brilliant at building athletes' self-confidence, self-esteem, sense of competence, and even competitiveness, while at the same time, fostering camaraderie and allegiance, the building blocks of "team spirit." Cultivating competitiveness along with team spirit takes some talent, and one trick lies in coaches' knack for handling competitiveness. They do not squelch it, nor do they inflate it. They find healthy ways to channel it. Very carefully, they develop the drive to win by encouraging each athlete's personal ambition.

One technique that is used almost universally by coaches is training up ambition by driving each athlete to compete against himself. Coaches push their charges toward achieving goals that are unique to each individual member of the team by demanding each athlete's "personal best." Every day, coaches challenge their athletes to beat yesterday's records. Every sprinter knows his fastest time, every hurdler knows his highest jump, and every basketball player knows his record for slam dunks. And in the daily grind of training, each team member is challenged to out-perform *himself.*

Like coaches, parents can work toward two distinct goals: building up each child's identity and developing both of them as members of a team, in this case, a family team. Even in our highly competitive Western culture, these aims are not mutually exclusive. It *is* possible to have competitive children who also like each other. If a pair of siblings seems to thrive on competition, parents need to recognize that such spiritedness is not necessarily unhealthy. Certainly, as the historian Peter Stearns of Carnegie Mellon University notes, the notion that there are healthy aspects to competition is hardly a new idea. If channeled wisely, competition can be a source of great achievement. Equally important, however, children need to be encouraged to compete against themselves, not just against each other. Most parents know that children should not be compared with each other, but what they often miss is that there is nothing wrong with comparing an individual child with himself. The road toward self-discovery has been well traveled by individuals striving to surpass only themselves.

Of course, a child's achievements need not be athletic, or anywhere near championship level. Whatever the challenge, wherever the arena of achievement, children simply need to feel that they can succeed. No child ever developed a healthy identity through constant exposure to failure and shame. Giving a child an attainable goal in any area yields pride and fuels a healthy sense of self-worth. On the other hand, when set too low, challenges are no longer challenges. They are just dull chores.

Children can be encouraged to surpass themselves in any number of ways, and finding activities in which a child can shine is no small part of the equation. Young children thrive particularly on challenges to surpass themselves in tasks that suggest being grown up and independent. If one day a child "read" one storybook, parents could congratulate him and suggest "reading" two storybooks the next day. If a youngster was able one day to button his sweater, parents could smile with pride and suggest he try to zipping up a jacket next, or tying his shoelaces. Challenging a young child's ability to entertain and care for an infant can be exceptionally gratifying. A two-year-old would be delighted to beat his own record for getting laughs out of a baby by inventing new ways of making silly faces. A three-year-old would love to teach a baby how to take two steps, after having last shown her how to take only one. Through early competition with themselves, children learn that their successes can occur at no one else's expense. Rather, their triumphs are as much a benefit to themselves as to those whom they have helped, such as their siblings. With this early discovery there arises a strong sense of self, in addition to budding "team spirit."

As children get a little older, parents can introduce some competition between siblings. Done right, this can serve as a superb outlet for competitiveness, and much enjoyment can be derived from these gamelike activities. A spirit of playful competition will enliven even the most mundane ones. Ordinary forms of competition, as in "last-one-upstairs-is-a-rotten-egg," create enormous excitement. Remarkably, they do so even though "winners" do not even get to win a prize. As long as each child has a fair chance of winning, which can take some finagling, and the stakes are not too high, competition can be immensely stimulating. And a spirit of sportsmanship and camaraderie will ensue. If parents and other family members are willing to enter into the competition, the outcome can be quite rewarding. The sensation of the Kennedy family's tradition of after-dinner football, with family members plus dinner guests included, is legendary.

Entertainment Fights

Entertainment fights exist because fights are a source of intellectual stimulation. In this sense, they serve as entertainment and are usually motivated by boredom. When life gets tedious, targeting a victim is a convenient way of initiating social interaction. True, the interaction is not friendly, but sometimes even unfriendly interaction is better than no interaction. Entertainment fights also help alleviate hunger, fatigue, being too hot or too cold, and other types of physical discomfort. In these situtions, the intellectual stimulation provided through fighting serves to distract children from whatever happens to be bothering them.

Older children certainly, ought to be able to figure out that if they are bored, they should go dig up something to do; if they are cold, they can put on a sweater; and if they are hungry, they should eat. Such effective action, however, is quite beyond the capabilities of young children, who often cannot even pinpoint the source of their discomfort, let alone take proper action. Even inquiring into whether a toddler feels hungry, tired, or cold, will often yield "no" in response. They also have lower tolerances for discomfort, and time seems to operate in slow motion. So aggression will easily erupt, as, for example, when an overheated two-year-old has to wait in line longer than two seconds for access to a water fountain. If the target of aggression happens to be a sibling, then the hostility will be thought of as sibling rivalry. But, to be more accurate, the hostility is more attributable to normal crankiness than brotherly love, or the lack of it. Taking care of a young child's physical and intellectual needs helps alleviate most of these sorts of fights.

Where Love Goes Wrong

When siblings quarrel, knowing what action to take requires knowing what brought on the conflict. Admittedly, this isn't always easy. Fights driven by jealousy, frustration, dominance, and entertainment are unique in their origins. Unfortunately, however, the fights are not unique in appearance. Actually, they can look quite alike. As a result, well-intentioned parents regularly employ the wrong kinds of intervention techniques. The worst, and most typical, mistake is offering assurances of love inappropriately. As a consequence, parental involvement often leads to an escalation of sibling conflict rather than harmony and peace.

So how can a confused and beleaguered parent disentangle the various motives behind sibling rivalry, and offer love, but only when appropriate? The safest rule of thumb is this: When in doubt about the source of conflict between siblings, proceed by considering motives starting from the last item on the list, entertainment fights.

Step One. Intervene between squabbling children by first asking whether any child is in discomfort. Is there a child who is bored, hungry, tired, hot, cold, or suffering from an upset stomach, diaper rash, or teething? It may simply be that a child has spent too many hours in front of a TV or computer monitor, or too much time in an overcrowded child care environment, and is exploding with excess energy and feelings of containment. It need not be both children who are in discomfort; one cranky child is enough to set off a storm. With young children, in particular, it is all too easy to underestimate the amount of aggression attributable to discomfort and boredom. Just remember that the physical needs of toddlers are substantial.

Even if they actually possess the vocabulary necessary for expressing themselves, young children are often unable to recognize the source of their discomfort, let alone articulate it to adults, or find a solution. When asked why he pushed his sister, no three-year-old will report that he was feeling out of sorts due to his molars coming in. Moreover, it is important to take care of discomfort early, before minor crankiness escalates into vicious behavior. Obviously, a tired, hungry, bored, or overheated toddler is not going to be receptive to a lecture on brotherly love. Even a show of parental attention will be a waste of time if what is needed is a meal, a nap, a cool bath, or some fresh air and exercise.

· · ·

Step Two. If the problem behavior is still unresolved by this level of intervention, move on to the next step, and consider dominance as the driving force behind sibling rivalry. Explore ways of challenging each child individually to out-perform himself. This takes some insight into a child, knowing what makes him tick. In other words, parents need to take some time to get to know a child and figure out what kinds of challenges are interesting, and what level of a challenge is high enough to be stimulating and attainable, but not so easily attainable as to be boring. Sometimes all that a parent needs to do is act as scorekeeper. Like a good coach, recalling a child's records for successful basketball shots, hop-scotch hops, frisbee catches, chin-ups, rope jumps, and books read can work wonders. Using a kitchen timer to help set records for speed works great.

Other times, parents can teach children games and sports to play against one another. If children are closely spaced, and thus fairly equal matches for each other, it is especially easy to cultivate competition and companionship through activities that require twosomes. Board games, card games, playing on a seesaw, ball games of pitch-and-catch, badminton and tennis are all impossible to play alone, and loads of fun with a buddy. Through these activities, children develop social skills, such as taking turns and good sportsmanship, which make them attractive play partners later with friends and peers outside the home. If children want to compete simply for the sake of competing, then find an activity they both like, and channel their competitiveness productively. Show them how to win and lose graciously. Remember, too, that mild teasing is part of the fun, and part of life. A sense of humor and learning how to laugh at oneself has rescued many from despair. Keep in mind that fights involve *two* children, and sometimes both children may have hot temperaments, in which case, getting the hang of channeling competitiveness may be the only chance of beating a lifetime of fallout.

Dominance fights, like entertainment fights, are not resolved by parents' offering assurances of love. Children involved in these fights are striving to know who they are and what they can achieve. They already know that they have achieved their parents' love, and they also know that parental love is not sufficient for their emotional well-being. At best, further assurances of maternal or paternal love will temporarily provide comfort by diverting attention from the true source of conflict. At worst, gushing love can suggest a parent's hubris in thinking that her love is so wonderful and all important that it can satisfy every possible emotional need in a child, while forgetting that children have psychological needs beyond those that can be fixed by parental love, even if the love is genuine. A parent being overly impressed with her own love can leave a child, already stranded with unmet identity needs, also feeling dismissed, angry that no one is willing to bother inquiring into what is *really* bothering him, and even feeling disdainful toward parental love altogether.

Step Three. If children are still in conflict, proceed to the next level, and address the possibility of frustration. Examine precisely what a child is craving, and then ask yourself where this expectation came from. Sometimes parents feel as though their children are constantly making demands for everything. But this perception is usually mistaken and also unjust in that it reflects an underestimation of parents' child-rearing skills. For example, children do not whine over being denied the privilege of playing in traffic. Remarkably, one never hears a three-year-old pleading for just one more chance to run in front of on-coming cars. Many children are curious about the experience of running in front of moving vehicles. Indeed, one sees children attempting it all the time. But curious children know that there is no point in begging for this privilege. Even children who have never been hit by a car, or have never experienced a traffic accident, understand that running in the street is forbidden. Children are not born with this knowledge. Rather, the knowledge has been acquired through parents who have made it clear that such a request would be denied. In fact, they made it so clear, that every child knows that any whining, negotiating, or uncivil behavior would undoubtedly result in a failure to produce a parent's change of heart. No exceptions. Case closed.

Children are amazingly adept at figuring out whether there is any room to maneuver around parental orders. They rarely waste time fussing over things they know they cannot have. On the other hand, they will invest enormous effort in kicking up a fuss if they think they have even a slim chance of success. And, although parents are quite capable of being consistent when it comes to setting limits in some instances, such as playing in traffic, they can be miserably inconsistent when setting limits in other instances. Setting limits regarding what children can have relative to their siblings is a common weak point. Parents have difficulty with this particular issue because they tend to interpret a child's demand for more attention as a sign of a child feeling unloved. But even children who know they are adored will want more attention, or, better yet, more attention than their siblings. If a child can sway a parent into thinking that he has been cheated out of love, he will then be lavished with a disproportionate amount of attention. This will, of course, only precipitate payback behavior from a sibling. And the poor parent will never hear the end of it.

The main solution strategy is to decide whether a child's demand for more loving attention is due to his feeling unloved, or due to greediness for more than his share of love. This can be a tough call. Think it through carefully. If parents judge that the child knows, deep down, that he is loved and loved fairly, then parents must simply have faith in this decision and act on it. Do not waffle. Parents who are guilt ridden and second-guessing themselves are easy prey for squabbling siblings who know, beyond doubt, that they are both loved equally. Sometimes, even after deciding that a child is fully aware of being loved, parents are still disinclined to show a sufficient level of firmness. Despite their decision not to give in, they find it difficult to resist offering love in response to sibling aggression. One trick parents can use in order to hold steadfast is to imagine that the child who has just slugged his sibling instead ran into oncoming traffic. This technique of using imagery can be quite helpful in trimming any leanings toward wimpiness.

At the same time, parents need to do their best to be consistent and fair in doing out attention. The easiest way to fairly allocate resources, such as parental attention, is to treat children exactly the same. In reality, this is impossible. Still, the closer the age difference between children, the easier it is to create perceptions of fairness by offering treatment that is, more or less, equal. Parents of twins, like child care givers and teachers working with same-age groups, have the easiest time dividing up resources fairly. This notwithstanding, children of different ages can learn to live with some variation in how they're treated, and in the process they eventually develop compassion and the ability to share. They can even learn to share parental attention. But these lessons are hard for young children to acquire without parents' commitment to being fair, even if unequal, having confidence in their allocation of resources, and then sticking to their decisions. In any case, these are situations that call for parental assurances, not of love, but of fairness. Given the right encouragement, children come to develop trust in their parents' pronouncements of what is fair.

Step Four. If even these efforts fail to reduce conflicts between siblings, consider jealousy as a possible motive for sibling conflict. In cases where a child truly fears that he is unloved or unequally loved, providing assurances of love are in order. But remember, even if parental love is expressed at an appropriate time, sometime *after* an aggressive incident has taken place, it needs to be offered in measured amounts. Otherwise, it will backfire. Unfortunately, parents regularly underestimate the damage that can be done by offering too much love. By giving a child love and reassurance right after he has just clobbered his baby brother, two things happen. First, the aggressive child feels reassured of love, jealousy is dampened, and jealousy fights subside. Second, the child develops the expectancy of receiving love for clobbering his brother. And when he again clobbers his baby brother, and parental reactions do not turn out as favorably as expected, he becomes frustrated and angry, and frustration fights ensue. In sum, frustration takes over from jealousy, and one problem has been replaced by another, of at least equal magnitude.

This pattern of jealousy being replaced by frustration is probably the most common method for intensifying sibling rivalry. Even when assurances of love are called for, and appropriately timed, the level of extra attention that a parent gives a jealous child must be carefully measured. Assurances need to be generous enough to reassure the child that he is loved equally, but parents cannot go overboard either. Otherwise, a child will come to expect that every time the baby takes a nap, Mommy will be available for two hours of exclusive attention and play. If this level of attention is beyond what Mommy can offer on a regular basis, inflated expectations can arise, leading to greediness for attention, and again resulting in frustration. Long after a child has been thoroughly assured of being loved, antagonism between siblings can be fueled by frustration due to inflated expectations of attention.

In sum, when the source of conflict is unfathomable, parents will often try offering love as the default mechanism for bringing about peace. But sibling conflict does not automatically merit reassurances of parental love. Keep in mind that conflict between siblings can be driven by a variety of motives, and fights attributed to "sibling rivalry" often have little to do with fears of being unloved or unequally loved by parents. Siblings who are enemies can be children who are deeply beloved by their parents, and well aware of it. If a child truly feels threatened with the loss of parental love, then, and only then, reassurances are warranted. In these instances, offer extra love only sometime after the aggressive incident has taken place. Offer it generously, but within reason, and only as a last resort.

These four steps should help reduce conflict between siblings, but that's only half the story. Children who don't fight may *not* be friends. In some families, nonquarrelsome siblings, even children who love their parents, can "get along" by being total strangers to each other. The risk for this climate of indifference is especially great for widely spaced children of different genders. So, raise *your* expectations. Expect more than merely an absence of jealousy and aggression. Lessened animosity is only an initial step toward the goal of establishing the relationship we wish for in our children.

Smell the Roses

Many parents do not know the answer to the question, What do siblings do when they are *not* fighting? For some parents, concerns over sibling rivalry are so overriding, they overshadow less easily noted events, such as sibling harmony. Other times, parents are so relieved by having a few moments of peace, they wish simply to savor them, uninterrupted. Still others are afraid that if they dared to do anything at all, even peek at the children, it would unbalance the shaky truce. Or, parents are just so busy, they do not get involved unless a child is shrieking for Mommy or Daddy. This pattern results in what is perhaps the greatest mistake that parents make in raising children: overreacting to negative behavior and underreacting to positive behavior.

Preventing Sibling Rivalry
Strategy Six

Handle conflict between children by first inquiring into whether it has been motivated by jealousy—feeling less loved than a sibling by parents—or if it is rooted in a different source of contention—frustration, identity issues, or physical needs. Reserve your assurance of love *only* for conflict instigated by jealousy; provide it sometime *after* hostility has been dealt with firmly, and offer it generously but within reason.

Spend time together with children when they are at peace and when *you* are at peace. Your enjoyment of them will nourish their enjoyment of each other. It will breathe friendship into their relationship, and set up the bond that can continue to grow throughout life.

Insight into a relationship requires more than understanding what makes it fail. It also requires recognizing what makes it work. Often, when we conjure up images of our young children being "perfect," we think of them in some spectacular setting, such as the beach, on a sunny day, frolicking in the waves or blissfully building castles in the sand. This popular image is somewhat deceptive. It tends to suggest that children cannot be perfect unless they are in some idyllic setting, like an island resort.

Actually, very little in the "ideal" setting is directly responsible for bringing about wonderful behavior in children. Moreover, the one feature of the beach setting that does, in fact, stand out in this capacity has more to do with spectacular qualities called forth in parents than in children. In the very same scenario where we visualize our little darlings, gleefully splashing about in the waves, we also imagine ourselves. Our imaginary selves are not exhausted, frazzled, and consumed with guilt. We are not overwhelmed by cooking dinner, as we talk to a sales rep on the phone, while trying to balance our checkbooks, with worries over having just bounced a check and guilt over not being in a family mood. In the dream scenario, we are calm and unhassled. Our lives are simple. All we have to do is play the role of lifeguard, which requires little more than simply watching our children. We are seated in comfortable lounge chairs, basking in the sunlight and in the sound of our children's laughter above the waves. We sit and gaze at them fondly, admiring them and ourselves for being such capable parents.

If there is a secret to understanding our young children's *good* behavior, it lies in appreciating what we, as parents, are doing while our children are well behaved. Are we there? If so, *how* are we there? If children feel that the only way to get parental attention is through misbehavior, then this is the behavior they will choose to display. The fact that the evoked parental response might not be pleasant is quite secondary. To young children, irate parents are better than no parents. Children require a great deal of attention; they need to be organized, entertained, and supervised. As any child care worker, teacher, and coach of young children knows, things fall apart fast when adults are remote.

At the same time, the presence of a parent does not require the parent's constant involvement. Being there is what counts, especially if parents appear relaxed and happy. The magical image of the beach scenario often includes parents who are playful, but they are not playmates. Mostly, it simply includes parents being casually watchful and looking pleasantly unstressed. To young children, this tells them that they are a source of pleasure to their parents. It means too, that they have the freedom to do their own thing, as well as confidence in knowing that they have easy access to a parent, if necessary.

Being close by and available, parents are able to preempt most fights and handle disagreements before they deteriorate into war.

It allows parents the opportunity to manage squabbles preventively by occasionally intervening on a young child's behalf. Because of having witnessed exactly what transpired without having to extract the "truth" from children's verbal recollections, it is a simple and effective way of handling disagreements. Over the course of childhood, children's requirements for supervision are reduced drastically. The last thing any teenager wants while at the beach is a loving parent hovering over him protectively. Even school-age children, however, report that they want more attention, but only from parents who are relaxed and in a good mood.

It is true that vacations provide wonderful opportunities for parents to unwind and take part in their children's lives. Still, the lovely behavior commonly seen in siblings at the beach is behavior that children are capable of displaying elsewhere. Young children can be enjoyed in many different, and less exotic, settings. With relaxed and happy parents, they can be enjoyed at the park; on bike rides, picnics, and walks; while visiting family and friends; and certainly at home. Moreover, as children are enjoyed by their parents, they learn to be enjoyed by each other. And in this emotional climate, sibling friendships blossom.

It should not be necessary for you to be on vacation in order to have the time and frame of mind to enjoy your children. Take a close look at what your children are doing when they are *not* fighting. You might be pleasantly surprised to discover that much of the time young siblings get along together quite nicely.

Chapter Ten

Jealousy Profiles of Toddlers and Young Children

John Travolta and Jett

"He's watched *Grease*," Travolta says. "Not the whole thing; he doesn't have the attention span. I've showed him two musical numbers, *Greased Lightning* and *You're the One that I Want*. He loves it. He loves *Look Who's Talking*, too, but when there's a scene where I have another kid in my arms, or a scene where I kiss Kirstie [Alley], forget it. WAAAAAAH! He doesn't like that at all."

Of course, most children do *not* turn on their television sets only to find Daddy, much less Daddy kissing some strange lady and baby. Undoubtedly, Jett Travolta's experience is not exactly typical for two-year-olds. This report, however, does highlight the fact that sibling rivalry is only one instance that arouses jealousy. Even though early jealousy is commonly displayed between siblings, it is not limited solely to situations involving blood relatives. In this

instance, rivalry is induced by complete strangers, suggesting that jealousy emerges in love relationships even without a history of disrupted household routines, competition, or displacement.

The scenario also illustrates that jealousy can be evoked by fathers. Jett, who loves to see his dad smiling while singing and dancing, knows that something is awry when Daddy is smiling at a stranger in his arms. Not only is jealousy induced here by a father, but this father shows a pattern of mixed reactions, which reflect paternal sensitivity, similar to maternal sensitivity, to infant jealousy's mixed messages. Though he deplores Jett's fussing, Mr. Travolta seems more than willing to share this tidbit of personal information with reporters. Certainly, he does not appear to be embarrassed by Jett's hot temperament, perhaps because he regards his son's jealousy as a tribute to their loving father-son relationship.

In addition, the episode shows the ease with which jealousy can be aroused in toddlers. That images on screen can elicit jealousy, even though they are not live, suggests how well-formed jealousy is by the time infants reach toddlerhood. Apparently, it does not take much for a wise two-year-old to detect hanky-panky. Because of the ease with which jealousy can be evoked, it can be aroused vigorously, yet unintentionally and unthinkingly. Consequently, adults sometimes misidentify jealousy in distraught, preverbal children, as depicted in the next, more typical, instance of early jealousy, where it will also become clear that such emotionality is not limited to children of movie stars.

Three Mothers and a Director

It was "Trip Day" at the Willow Lake Preschool for children, two to five years of age. This event was scheduled for each Thursday of the four-week day-camp program by the director, Donna. On the first Thursday, the little campers hopped onto the bus and headed for the petting zoo. Of course, taking young children on an outing requires every precaution, so parents were invited to come along as chaperones. Besides, thought Donna, what a delightful occasion for parents and children to share some quality time together.

One of the parents was Mrs. Abrams, mother of one son, a two-year-old named Andy. An attractive and immaculately dressed woman, Mrs. Abrams came to Donna's attention early in the day, as she cheerfully led her jolly flock to see the llamas. With Andy and his buddy Jill on her right, and Joey on her left, the hand-holding little foursome was off to a fine start. Not long afterward, as they were moving on to see the sheep, Donna noticed that Mrs. Abrams now had only two children, not three. Apparently, Joey had been passed along to his teacher, Miss Sara.

Mrs. Abrams was now a little less lively, and perhaps a bit fatigued, but intact. Twenty minutes later, another check on Mrs. Abrams revealed that she now had only one child, her own son. Jill was back with her teacher, Miss Beth. Though still in reasonably good shape, Mrs. Abram's initial perkiness had definitely begun to fade.

That perhaps three toddlers, or even two toddlers, had been a bit much for some inexperienced mothers, was Donna's only passing thought about the incident. Still, after a while, Donna again checked back to see how Mrs. Abrams was holding up. Donna was expecting to find an angelic-looking child in the midst of the group, happily escorted by a devoted mother, all to himself. But it was not like that at all. Having drifted behind the group, Mrs. Abrams was now strenuously hoisting Andy over the water fountain. Five minutes later, she was straining to lift him to see the ponies, and then again to see the goats. Ten minutes later they were seen heading for the bathroom. Next time, they were at the concession stand, first for ice cream, then soda. After that, Mrs. Abrams was seen chasing her son, who was bolting for a door marked Danger. The water-fountain concession-stand bathroom-chase sequence seemed to repeat itself several more times. Suddenly, Andy was heard shrieking wildly. He was throwing garbage at the goats, and taunting them. Then he began jumping up and down, quite out of control. It took three members of the staff and one security guard to restrain him, while a crowd gathered round to observe the mayhem, pityingly. By this time, Mrs. Abrams had obviously reached her breaking point. Her face was flushed, her makeup smeared, her hair a wreck, and she was babbling to herself, tearfully.

One more check on Mrs. Abrams revealed that she was nowhere to be found. With some alarm, Donna scoured every animal pen, concession stand, water fountain, and rest room. Finally, the delinquent pair was discovered at the bus. Mrs.

Abrams was collapsed in a heap on one of the benches, her clothing smeared with ice cream and soda, and plastered onto her with perspiration. At this stage, she looked frazzled to the point of appearing deranged. Her eyes were unfocused and she was too worn out to speak above a whisper. She looked at Donna, her face crimson with shame, and sobbed, "I don't know what got into him. He's never like this." Donna and the bus driver looked at each other, rolled their eyes, and smiled cynically. Then Donna walked away shaking her head, wondering why parenting classes are not mandatory. In the meantime, though somewhat subdued, Andy's unrelenting whining and fussing could still be heard in the background. In a little while, the rest of the group started to assemble at the bus. Donna noted that everyone looked fine, although Miss Sara and Miss Beth, bringing up the rear with extra toddlers in tow, were overheard mumbling something about incompetent mothers and spoiled children.

A week went by and another trip was in store for the little campers. This Thursday's event was a tot-sized amusement park. The day got off to a wonderful start as the bus loaded up with excited toddlers, and of course, their composed mothers. Mrs. Brown, mother of bright-eyed Jessica, hopped on with enthusiasm, which did not foretell the day's events. Things started to fall apart quickly. Almost immediately after having arrived at the park, Mrs. Brown shed her extra charges, Lauren and Jamie. Next, she and Jessica were found straggling behind the group. Instead of enjoying the rides and the company of the other children, the Browns were somewhere between the parking lot and a back alley. The couple never actually made it to the rides. Instead, they were preoccupied by various detours to the concession stand, rest rooms, and water fountains.

Donna sized up the situation, and when Jessica's fussing eventually escalated into a temper tantrum at the concession stand over having been served a hot dog with mustard instead of ketchup, Donna was not surprised. She was also not alarmed when it was learned, shortly afterward, that the Browns were missing. Except for the fact that Mrs. Brown's outfit was smeared with mustard and ketchup, instead of ice cream and soda, she looked quite like Mrs. Abrams had appeared, one week earlier, when Donna found her in the bus in a state of collapse. With a look of deep embarrassment, again mirroring last week's look, Mrs. Brown whimpered in dismay, "I don't know what got into him. He's never like this." The déjà vu experience of hearing these phrases repeated, exactly as they had been uttered last week, left Donna perplexed. She looked at Mrs. Brown quizzically. Could it be true that these infants really had never before behaved in this manner, she pondered to herself as she walked away.

The following Thursday's trip had barely gotten under way when it started to became clear that the victim of the week was going to be Mrs. Cruz, mother of two-year-old Devon. This time Donna caught on and intervened early enough to at least forestall a major showdown. At the close of the day, by the bus, of course, Donna approached Mrs. Cruz and said, "You don't know what got into him. And he's never like this. Right?" Mrs. Cruz's reply, "Yes! How did you know?" and the change of expression on her face, from shame, to wide-eyed disbelief, and then gratitude, was something Donna never forgot.

The fourth, and final, week's trip was canceled due to bad weather.

The children in this account were extremely upset, yet the source of their disturbance was not immediately obvious. To the mothers, the bus driver, and the overtaxed teaching staff, it simply appeared as though these were badly behaved, frustrated, and overly indulged "terrible twos." At first, Donna shared their view. But her impression started to change upon hearing two mothers utter the exact same words, "I don't know what got into him. He's *never* like this." With this, Donna began to speculate that the mothers were speaking the truth, and that the out-of-control behaviors she had seen in these infants were not simply cases of frustration.

By the time a third mother showed the same pattern of dismay at her infant's behavior, Donna had begun to recognize that the tantrums she had witnessed may have been triggered by jealousy. By this time, it had started to become clear that during the field trips, the infants had found themselves in a situation where they were being asked to share their mothers with other children. Since these particular toddlers did not have siblings, none had ever experienced anything comparable to this type of situation, and none had acquired coping mechanisms for dealing with the dilemma. And being only preverbal two-year-olds, they also had no way of knowing that their mothers' attention to other children was only temporary. In fact, the situation that these infants found themselves facing did not differ greatly from that faced by children in family settings. Like toddlers confronted with a new baby sibling, these young campers coped by distracting their mothers from the other children, by demanding tremendous amounts of attention, and by monopolizing all of their weary mothers' energies.

It is interesting that this pattern of extreme distress was evident only among the youngest children in the group. Even three-year-olds would already have acquired enough language to comprehend that this was to be only a temporary imposition. They would have to share their mothers just for one day. It is also notable, thankfully, that extreme responses were not seen in all the young infants. Only the two-year-olds with hot temperaments showed these intense reactions.

The mothers' surprise at their toddlers' angry behavior is understandable, yet unfortunate. Evidently, the mothers were dismayed by their infants' disgraceful behavior because they were unaccustomed to such angry demonstrations. Most likely, these hot babies were just as their mothers had described them, generally good natured and loving infants, not little terrors. Yet, had the mothers caught onto the fact that jealousy was at the root of their toddlers' disturbances, perhaps they might have been more effective in dealing with their infants' distress. The success of Donna's intervention on the third week suggests that a great deal of emotional turmoil might have been reduced, if not avoided entirely, had mothers addressed it as jealousy.

Oddly, adults are slow in recognizing jealousy in young infants, especially if it arises in struggles between infants who are not family members. Conversely, we are quick, sometimes too quick, in pointing to jealousy as a motive in conflicts that involve siblings, as illustrated in the following story.

The Biter

When Donna first heard about Billy, this bright-eyed, freckle-faced youngster was simply called "the biter." He was made known to Donna by his preschool's outgoing director, Rhonda, when Donna applied for the position being vacated by Rhonda. As if her conscience had forbidden her from concealing a major drawback to the position she had been trying so hard to sell, in the last moments of the interview a guilt-ridden Rhonda came out with the woeful admission that the school had one little problem, a biter. Rhonda's description of Billy was an eerie recollection of what appeared to her to be a normal three-year-old, who was occasionally, somehow, possessed by the devil. When least expected, despite being apparently unprovoked, this child would pick out an innocent victim, possibly even an infant, and attack. Rhonda conceded that the randomness, cruelty, and inexplicable nature of these acts had her bewildered and horrified. Certain that this had to be an exaggeration, and needing work badly, Donna took the job.

Within a week, the biter struck. Teeth marks were found on wailing Jessica's arm. Fortunately, no blood was drawn, thanks, in part, to Miss Kelley's lightening fast response. Nevertheless, chaos followed. The outraged parents of the victim, and the hysterical teachers, filled with guilt and recrimination, were equally adamant in demanding that Billy be dismissed from the school. When all this came to the attention of Billy's mother, Mrs. Brown, she broke down. She begged Donna to give Billy one more chance, sobbing as she confessed that Billy had already been expelled from three other preschools in the past six months. For Donna, this was the first time it had ever occurred to her that anyone as young as three years of age could have already experienced so much school failure.

Mrs. Brown went on to explain that she, her husband, and Billy were in therapy over her son's "mean streak." Since the onset of Billy's biting had coincided with the birth of her second child, Bonnie, his aggressive behavior had been interpreted by the therapist as an act of "displaced sibling rivalry" resulting from his feeling unloved. Mrs. Brown had been informed that in order to vent his jealousy, Billy had been targeting infants and children at the child care center, instead of his baby sister. She added that she was confident that a few more months of therapy would help Billy work through his jealousy successfully. Additionally, she had been emphatically advised that a stable child care environment was imperative to Billy's mental health and that any change in child care arrangements could be seriously detrimental to his recovery from the trauma of his sister's arrival.

Unpopular as it was with some of the parents and staff, Donna gave in and allowed Billy another chance. This time, however, Donna herself kept an eye on the little biter. She discovered that most of the time Billy was a great kid, well liked by his peers and generally not unlike them. But she also noticed that if Billy was one of thirty children on the playground, one staff member was assigned to the task of watching Billy, and only Billy, while the other teacher watched the remaining twenty-nine children. If he was in a class of a dozen children, the teacher managed eleven of them, and the aide watched Billy. It soon became apparent that at any point on any given day, through the variety of indoor and outdoor activities and shift changes, at least one set of eyes was steadily fixed on Billy. At the same time, Billy seemed to be keeping tabs on the staff. Every so often, he would stop whatever he was doing and carefully scan the room to check whether he was indeed receiving someone's undivided attention. And if Billy happened to catch a teacher with her guard down, trouble was shortly at hand, unless, of course, he was intercepted by a sharp-eyed member of the staff. There were a number of close calls.

Donna also spent some time getting to know Mrs. Brown. This lady turned out to be a charming and lovely woman, and an exceptionally devoted mother. Mrs. Brown explained that she had done everything imaginable to "prepare" Billy for Bonnie's arrival. After having read books to him about becoming a sibling, taken him with her on doctor visits, and given him as many gifts as the baby, she found his aggressive behavior incomprehensible. When Donna asked Mrs. Brown to describe Billy's behavior at home toward his baby sister, Mrs. Brown lit up. Glowingly, she reported that Billy adored Bonnie, and that he loved to entertain her. In fact, making Bonnie giggle was the high point of his day. She also mentioned that Billy had actually started biting children sometime before the baby's arrival.

The following day, after a particularly close call, in which a child was left just short of suffering teeth marks, Donna decided that Billy was due for a "promotion." Despite recommendations that Billy should remain in familiar surroundings, with a teacher to whom he had become closely attached, Billy was moved from the "toddler" room to the "preschool" room. In this process, Billy stayed in the same school, but went from being the largest child in a class of two- and three-year-olds, to being the smallest child in a class of four- and five-year-olds. Being little for his age, Billy suddenly found himself smaller than even the tiniest girl in the class.

Not a single incident—no biting, no aggression of any sort, not even a close call—was reported following the promotion, although there was some mention of roughhousing in the preschool room in which a girl sat on top of Billy and refused to budge for some extended period of time. No one ever found out why. When asked how things were going at home, Mrs. Brown reported that home life was just fine, as it had always been. The Browns terminated therapy shortly afterward, and their lives went back to normal.

Whereas the previous account had depicted an instance where two-year-old campers' jealousy was mistaken for frustration, Billy's story is a case in which a child's frustration was mistaken for jealousy. Disentangling jealousy from frustration is problematic. In the case of Billy, it was easy to assume that his hostility was inspired by jealousy simply by looking no further than the timing of the onset of his aggression, and by conveniently ignoring the fact that his biting at least in its initial form, had actually begun sometime before the baby's arrival. Regrettably, no one had ever bothered to ask what, besides jealousy, could have motivated such objectionable behavior.

What Donna learned, through observing Billy and listening to his mother, was inconsistent with Mrs. Brown's "mean streak" interpretation, Rhonda's "possessed-by-the-devil" reading, and the therapist's diagnosis of "displaced jealousy." Donna found Mrs. Brown to be a kind and concerned parent, someone not likely to raise the kind of vicious child who takes pleasure in harming young children. She also learned that Billy was popular with his preschool buddies, attached to his teacher, and showed only playful affection toward Bonnie at home. Certainly, this was not the profile one would expect of a deeply troubled child.

Most important, Donna discovered that Billy had somehow come upon a fool-proof formula for seeing to it that he was at the center of attention at school. With the reputation of being a biter, Billy found himself assured of enjoying constant attention throughout the course of the day. Donna deduced that Billy's aggressive behavior was the result of his learning, perhaps accidentally at some earlier point in one of his previous preschools, that he could get maximal levels of adult attention merely by taking a chomp out of some smaller child.

Putting all of this together, Donna came upon the realization that this was not an instance of a child lashing out with jealousy due to feeling unloved or from trauma brought on by a new sibling's arrival. Rather, Billy was just a regular little terror, frustrated by finding himself deprived of his teacher's undivided attention. Truth in this determination was born out by the positive outcome of Donna's firm course of action. When placed in a class with bigger children, Billy soon discovered that soft targets were no longer easy to come by. And in the process, he also learned that easy targets were not a necessity. Apparently, he could get along even without nonstop attention from the staff. Once jealousy was ruled out as the motive for his hostility, his improvement was rapid; in fact it was almost instantaneous. One can only guess what progress Billy would have made, left to "work through" his jealousy in the comfortable setting of a class filled with younger and smaller children. Clearly, confusing frustration for jealousy can have serious consequences for young children and their families, not to mention their victims.

Mr. and Mrs. Blake, and Tommy

By most people's account, Tommy was a fortunate child. He was born into a comfortable life with happily married parents, and, in particular, an exceptionally loving and involved father. Not a day went by without Mr. Blake spending some time with Tommy, taking a bike ride, reading books, or just horsing around on the living room carpet. Holidays were frequent, and often included fishing and boating trips, which Tommy loved. When he was four years old, a baby brother, Alfie, was born. Tommy had seen his mother's belly expand, and there had been much explaining and gift giving. But nothing had prepared him for the sense of abandonment he felt when he saw both parents immerse themselves in the new baby.

After an initial reaction of anger, Tommy fell into a state of sullenness, and there he stayed for a period of almost two years. During that time, he made no effort to get to know Alfie or to play with him. Despite his parents' attempts to draw him into the newly constructed family life, Tommy seemed to have no patience for the baby, whom he held responsible for his father's reduced energy and playfulness. Alfie turned two when Tommy entered first grade. Now that he was in elementary school and enrolled in baseball, Tommy had lots of friends and interests. He felt very grown up, and happier. By this time, he had slowly come round to being close to his dad once again. But the relationship with his father never went back to what it had been before his brother's arrival, and Tommy and Alfie were never to become close friends.

Losing the exclusive attention of one parent is difficult; losing this status from two parents can be doubly difficult. For some children, such extensive loss represents an almost insurmountable level of stress. A two-year period of adjustment is a very long time in a child's life. One can speculate that Tommy might have had an easier adjustment had his parents' level of attention been more consistent. Tommy received more parental attention than most children, even after Alfie was born. Still, what precipitated Tommy's reaction was the drop in attention, rather than the absolute amount of attention. Once a child has developed a level of expectancy, he will be disappointed if he receives anything less than what he is accustomed to, even if the lesser amount is still quite reasonable, or even generous, by most standards.

Unfortunately, parents can get too embroiled in the impossible task of equalizing attention between siblings, while remaining blind to the discrepancy between the levels of attention a firstborn receives before and after a newborn's arrival. Normally, this is achieved by making efforts to increase the amount of attention offered a firstborn after a second child arrives. Realistically, though, sometimes the task can be achieved only by decreasing the amount of attention given firstborns before a newborn is added to the family. This option becomes necessary if the early level of attention is extremely high, as in the case of Tommy, where both parents were highly indulgent, perhaps excessively. In instances like this, parents inadvertently create expectations that are so high, they are impossible to live up to once a second child arrives, thus setting up their firstborns for the crushing letdown that comes with having "false hopes."

Tommy was lucky in having parents who were patient and persistent in their efforts to reengage him in family life. Yet Tommy's failure to bond closely with his brother came as a disappointment to the Blakes. Quite possibly, his difficulty in coping with the drop in parental attention could have been buffered by the appeal of brotherly companionship. Unfortunately, this was precluded by age spacing, which failed to make companionship much of a possibility until it was too late for real friendship to form.

The richness that close spacing can bring to family life is eloquently portrayed in this final excerpt from a work by Anna Quindlen, Pulitzer Prize–winning columnist, and mother. This narrative is a gem, not only because accounts of closely spaced siblings are rare, but because siblings are so often depicted solely in shades of black and white. In this insightful essay, Quindlen takes note of her young sons at peace, but she sees them also while in conflict. Finally, her reflections on parenting closely spaced children parallel some of my own personal recollections. In particular, her words remind me of the faith I had in the emotional strength of my firstborn daughter, Alison, when she was just a toddler, and of my joy and wonder and at the good times and the extraordinary friendship that followed between her and my second-born child, Lyndia, another daughter, only twenty-two months younger.

Quindlen here compellingly invites what is brought out in most of us by reminders of the exquisite tenderness and touching friendship possible in young siblings—renewed hope for the future and faith in the goodness of mankind.

Irish Twins

My boys are what were once called Irish Twins; that is, I had them less than two years apart and far too close together for most people's comfort. I bought a double stroller and endured the stares of those who were clearly doing the math in their head. The year after the second was born is a blur to me, all diapers and spilt milk. There may have been no use crying about it, but cry they did.

I did this because I had a deep and enduring belief that two children born less than two years apart would become boon companions and lifelong friends, despite all the evidence I'd seen to the contrary. But this is indeed what happened. Quin could not remember life before Christopher, and Christopher had never had a life without Quin. Christopher used his walker to get as close to Quin as possible and, when permitted—and he usually was—to grab on to Quin's shirt and be dragged along in his wake. One of Quin's first words was "Cur," which became "Chrifer," which became "Christopher." They shared a room and, at night, little boy conversation that would come to us in fits and starts over the baby monitor.

Once Christopher was asked to write a paragraph about his best friend. Here is what he wrote: "My best frend is a boy namd Quin. He likes to play. He is a good drawr. He is my brother. He is nice. I like him."

It was what we in the trade call understatement. Not to mention effective. It made my heart rattle in the cage of my chest.

I read in one of my baby books once that it takes a child many, many months before he finally realizes that he is a separate entity from his mother, or, perhaps more important, that his mother is separate from him. Christopher learned that he and I were different people long before he learned that he and Quin were. I had a book on sibling rivalry that I bought and read during my second pregnancy, looking at Quin with drawn brows over its edge. Six months after Christopher was born I gave it away. What I needed was a book on sibling dependency.

Maybe sometimes this happens with siblings of different sexes; I'm not sure. The only times I've seen it it's been with same sex kids; sisters, brothers. Not always then, of course: I knew two sisters once not 18 months apart in age whose mother had been afraid to leave the room when they were small because she was afraid the elder would do physical damage to the younger. Whenever I looked at the elder girl I used to think of those Siamese fighting fish you see, swimming solitary, doing a slow fan dance with those iridescent tails in glass bowls in the pet shop. There's never more than one because they kill each other when they're together.

But that was not what happened with my sons. They played together fairly peacefully, held hands walking down the street once the double stroller had been outgrown. They could fight, too, and wrestle, try to pin one another down, demand "Uncle." Siblings like to do that, if they like each other: it is the one safe way of using your feet and your fists, if you're certain the other person doesn't secretly have murder in his heart.

They were playmates and confidants and I could almost see them, in their twenties, on the phone, having a beer in a bar, saying to one another, "What's up with Mom and Dad?" And sometimes when I saw the two of them, their heads bent together over a game, one dark, one fair, I felt that I had made a perfect world that would continue long after I was gone.

Two things happened to change that. One was that their sister was born, and their magic circle made her feel excluded, which made them feel bad and made me feel sad. But the second was that, as they grew older, the circle was no longer large enough to contain them, their ambition, their sense of adventure, of wanting to re-create and redefine themselves.

I use that plural pronoun as a kindness, but it is not really accurate. What really happened was that the elder wanted to set sail on the seas of the outside world, to make friends and influence people. It was always clear that he loved and cherished his brother; it was also clear that the bond between them was not sufficient to sustain him, once he got older, edgier, more drawn to the tightrope. One day the time came for him to go off to a different school, a school his younger brother had never visited, to make friends with boys his younger brother did not know and do things his younger brother had never done.

When the younger one went back to their old school that fall, he looked at the end of the day like a hot air balloon that had lost its flame and its fuel, crumpled and flat and earthbound. This was particularly noticeable as the elder soared.

I can't tell you how this story ends yet because I'm in the thick of it now. The younger has moved outside of himself and his family circle, too; he has begun to inflate again. The elder insists that he must join him at his new school. Their sister ricochets from one to another. Sometimes all three of them lie in the hammock stretched between two tall pines and talk for hours, spinning the fantasy stories they all three like, the eldest because he is clever; the second because he is creative, the third because the other two like to do this and let her in when she does.

They make a charmed circle of their own, the three of them swinging between the trees. I do not belong within it, but I recognize it. I think of climbing into the low-slung seat of my sister's sports car in California at the airport last year, a car I could never buy, given my life now, in a state where I will never live, with a woman I have not seen for a year. It is still so hard for me to think of her as a woman: I still worry about whether she has enough money, or enough furniture, or just enough. I still think of her as a girl, somehow, a baby.

But that is because she is always, first and foremost to me, my sister. There are no preliminaries, as she tears onto the freeway. (Is she careful enough? Does she have tickets? Insurance?) There is none of that small talk that breaks the ice with even our good friends. There is no ice to break. That is what it means to have brothers and sister, I suppose, in the last analysis: there is no ice to break.

References

Chapter One

6. They did so even if they did not have: Hart, S., Field, T., del Valle, C., & Letourneau, M. (1998). Infants protest their mothers attending to an infant-size doll. *Social Development, 7,* 54–61.

7. We don't infer that: Lewis, M., & Haviland, J. (1993). *Handbook of emotions.* New York: Guilford.

12. The triangular situations that: Mock, D., & Parker, G. (1997). *The evolution of sibling rivalry.* Oxford: Oxford University Press.

12. The triangular situations that: Mathes, E. (1991). A cognitive theory of jealousy. In P. Salovey (Ed.), *The psychology of jealousy and envy.* New York: Guilford.

13. All this takes a level of social: Lewis, M., & Saarni, C. (1985). *The socialization of emotions.* New York: Plenum.

13. Confirming suggestions based on: Dunn, J., Kendrick, C., & MacNamee, R. (1981). The reaction of first-born children to the birth of a sibling: Mothers' reports. *Journal of Child Psychology and Psychiatry, 22,* 1–18.

13. Confirming suggestions based on: Legg, C., Sherick, I., & Wadland, W. (1974). Reaction of preschool children to the birth of a sibling. *Child Psychiatry and Human Development, 5,* 3–39.

13. Confirming suggestions based on: Levy, D. (1934). Rivalry between children of the same family. *Child Study, 11,* 261.

13. Confirming suggestions based on: Clanton, G., & Kosins, D. (1991). Developmental correlates of jealousy. In P. Salovey (Ed.), *The psychology of jealousy and envy.* New York: Guilford.

13. Confirming suggestions based on: Hart, S., Field, T., Letourneau, M., & del Valle, C. (1998). Jealousy protests in infants of depressed mothers. *Infant Behavior and Development, 21,* 137–148.

13. Confirming suggestions based on: Jones, N., Hart, S., & Field, T. (2000, July). Infant jealousy and attachment patterns in infants of depressed mothers. In R. Draghi-Lorenz, Chair, *Jealousy in young infants: A new area of research.* Symposium conducted at the meeting of the 12th Biennial International Conference on Infant Studies, Brighton, UK.

16. Thus, an innate tendency toward shyness: Kagan, J., Arcus, D., & Snidman, N. (1993). The idea of temperament: Where do we go from here? In R. Plomin & G. McClearn (Eds.), *Nature, nurture, and psychology.* Washington, DC: American Psychological Association.

Chapter Two

23. We understand, for example: Lewis, M. (1993). The emergence of human emotions. In M. Lewis & J. Haviland (Eds.), *Handbook of emotions.* New York: Guilford.

23. Viewing jealousy as emerging from anger: Bridges, K. (1932). Emotional development in early infancy. *Child Development, 3,* 324–341.

25. We had discovered that even though: Hart, S. (1996, May). Mothers reinforce jealousy protest. In C. Bower, Chair, *Processes underlying jealousy.* Symposium conducted at the meeting of the Association for Behavior Analysis, San Francisco.

25. To explain this emotional mismatch: Hart, S. (2000, July). Adults' reactions to infant anger and jealousy. In R. Draghi-Lornez, Chair, *Jealousy in young infants: A new area of research.* Symposium conducted at the meeting of the 12th Biennial International Conference on Infant Studies, Brighton, UK.

26. Darwin kept an account: Darwin, C. (1877). A biographical sketch of an infant. *Mind, 7,* 285–294.

27. He characterized Doddy's frustration: Ekman, P. (1973). *Darwin and facial expression.* New York: Academic.

30. Jeff Bryson at San Diego University: Bryson, J. B. (1991). Modes of response to jealousy-evoking situations. In P. Salovey (Ed.), *The psychology of jealousy and envy.* New York: Guilford.

32. To find out more about mothers' reactions: Hart, S. (2000, July). Adults' reactions to infant anger and jealousy. In R. Draghi-Lorenz, Chair, *Jealousy in young infants: A new area of research.* Symposium conducted at the meeting of the 12th Biennial International Conference on Infant Studies, Brighton, UK.

33. Studies show that adults' greater jealousy: Buunk, B. (1982). Anticipated sexual jealousy: Its relationship to self-esteem, dependency, and reciprocity. *Personality and Social Psychology Bulletin, 8,* 310–316.

33. Again, it may be the case: Berscheid, E. (1983). *Emotion.* In H. H. Kelley, E. Berscheid, A. Christensen, J. H. Harvey, T. L. Huston, G. Levinger, E. McClintock, L. A. Peplau, & D. R. Peterson (Eds.), *Close relationships.* New York: Freeman.

33. Again, it may be the case: Pines, A., & Aaronson, E. (1983). Antecedents, correlates, and consequences of sexual jealousy. *Journal of Personality, 51,* 108–136.

34. Mothers taking weak action: Perozynski, L., & Kramer, L. (1999). Parental beliefs about managing sibling conflict. *Developmental Psychology, 35,* 489–499.

34. Mothers taking weak action: Commentary. (1999, March 22). *Time,* p. 91.

Chapter Three

36. Here is Burton White's often-cited description: White, B. (1995). The new first three years of life. New York: Fireside, p. 179.

37. Excellent studies, documenting infants' attachment: Schaffer, H., & Emerson, P. (1964). The development of social attachments in infancy. *Monographs of the Society for Research in Child Development, 29* (4).

38. Excellent studies documenting infants' attachment: Pederson, F., & Robson, K. (1969). Father participation in infancy. *American Journal of Orthopsychiatry, 39,* 466–472.

39. Almost every study on every different subgroup: Pleck, J. (1997). Paternal involvement: Levels, sources, and consequences. In M. Lamb (Ed.), *The role of the father in child development,* (3rd ed.). New York: Wiley.

39. Almost every study on every different subgroup: Hossain, Z., & Roopnarine, J. (1994). African-American fathers' involvement with infants: Relationship to their functional style, support, education, and income. *Infant Behavior and Development, 17,* 175–184.

40. Infants form attachments with their fathers: Easterbrooks, M. A., & Goldberg, W. (1984). Toddler development in the family: Impact of father involvement and parenting characteristics. *Child Development, 53,* 740–752.

41. Even in infancy, relationships are a two-way street: Lewis, M., & Rosenblum, L. (1974). *The effect of the infant on the caregiver.* New York: Wiley.

41. Twenty years ago, Michael Yogman: Yogman, M. (1981). Games fathers and mothers play with their infants. *Infant Mental Health Journal, 2,* 241–248.

41. As infants get a little bit older: Clarke-Stewart, K. (1978). And daddy makes three: The father's impact on mother and young child. *Child Development, 49,* 466–478.

41. As infants get a little bit older: Parke, R. (1979). Perspectives on father-infant interaction. In J. Osofsky (Ed.), *Handbook of infant development*. New York: Wiley.

41. This type of invigorating play: Pruett, K., & Litzenberger, B. (1992). Latency development in children of primary nurturing fathers: Eight-year follow-up. *Psychoanalytic Study of the Child, 4,* 85–101.

42. For example, Tiffany Field: Field, T. (1978). Interaction behaviors of primary versus secondary caretaker fathers. *Developmental Psychology, 14,* 183–184.

42. Many studies find that fathers: Sagi, A., Lamb, M., Shoham, R., Dvir, R., & Lewkowicz, K. (1985). Parent-infant interaction in families on Israeli kibbutzim. *International Journal of Behavioral Development, 8,* 273–284.

42. Many studies find that fathers: Frodi, A., Lamb, M., Hwang, C., & Frodi, M. (1983). Father-mother-infant interaction in traditional and nontraditional Swedish families: A longitudinal study. *Alternative Lifestyles, 5,* 142–163.

42. Moreover, mothers spend so much more time: Yarrow, L., MacTurk, R., Vietz, P., McCarthy, M., Klein, R., & McQuiston, S. (1984). Developmental course of parental stimulation and its relationship to mastery motivation during infancy. *Developmental Psychology, 20,* 492–503.

42. As leaders in the field of infancy research: Lamb, M., (1997). Fathers and child development: An introductory overview and guide. In M. Lamb (Ed.), *The role of the father in child development* (3rd ed.). New York: Wiley.

42. As leaders in the field of infancy research: Fogel, A. (1997). *Infancy: Infant, family, and society* (3rd ed.). Minneapolis/St. Paul: West.

42. As leaders in the field of infancy research: Bremner, J. G. (1994). *Infancy* (2nd ed.). Oxford: Blackwell.

43. At birth, an infant will prefer her mother's voice: DeCasper, A., & Prescott, P. (1984). Human newborns' perception of male voices: Preference, discrimination and reinforcing value. *Developmental Psychobiology, 17,* 481–491.

43. Trust in fathers develops at a slower pace: Lamb, M. (1977). The development of parental preferences in the first two years of life. *Developmental Psychology, 13,* 637–648.

43. Here is one father's candid: Kluger, B. (2000). *Return of the stork.* www.odaddy.com.

45. With the passage of time: Belsky, J., Gilstrap, B., & Rovine, M. (1984). The Pennsylvania Infant and Family Development Project: I. Stability and change in mother-infant and father-infant interaction in a family setting at one, three, and nine months. *Child Development, 55,* 692–705.

45. Cues, such as an infant's smiles: Lamb, M., Thompson, R., Gardner, W., & Charnov, E. (1985). *Infant-mother attachment: The origins and developmental significance of individual differences in Strange Situation behavior.* Hillsdale, NJ: Erlbaum.

References

45. Cues, such as an infant's smiles: Trivers, R. (1972). Parental investment and sexual selection. In B. Campbell (Ed.), *Sexual selection and the descent of man, 1871–1971*. Chicago: Aldine.

47. Surely, it comes as no surprise: Kendrick, C., & Dunn, J. (1980). Caring for a second baby: Effects on interaction between mother and firstborn. *Developmental Psychology, 16*, 303–311.

47. As Cecily Legg noted, some decades ago: Legg, C., Sherick, I., & Wadland, W. (1974). Reaction of preschool children to the birth of a sibling. *Child Psychiatry and Human Development, 5*, 3–39, p. 20.

47. This clinical observation was later upheld: Gottlieb, L., & Mendelson, M. (1990). Parental support and firstborn girls' adaptation to the birth of a sibling. *Journal of Applied Developmental Psychology, 11*, 29–48.

49. Still, if a father is somewhat delayed: Silverstein, L., & Auerbach, C. (1999). Deconstructing the essential father. *American Psychologist, 54*, 397–407.

50. Some studies show that girls are: Lamb, M. (1977). The development of parental preferences in the first two years of life. *Developmental Psychology, 13*, 637–648.

50. Others show that boys who will get into: Garcia, M., Shaw, D., Winslow, E., & Yaggi, K. (2000). Destructive sibling conflict and the development of conduct problems in young boys. *Developmental Psychology, 36*, 44–53.

50. Here, in the lingo of psychiatry: Stewart, R., Mobley, L., Van Tuyl, S., & Salvador, M. (1987). The firstborn's adjustment to the birth of a sibling: A longitudinal assessment. *Child Development, 58*, 341–355, p. 342.

51. Whenever studies have asked whether: Dunn, J., & Kendrick, C. (1982). *Siblings*. Cambridge, MA: Harvard University Press.

Chapter Five

64. For each level, it depicts: Hart, S., Field, T., del Valle, C., & Letourneau, M. (1998). Infants protest their mothers attending to an infant-size doll. *Social Development, 7*, 54–61.

64. For each level, it depicts: Hart, S., Field, T., Letourneau, M., & del Valle, C. (1998). Jealousy protests in infants of depressed mothers. *Infant Behavior and Development, 21*, 137–148.

64. For each level, it depicts: Hart, S., Field, T., & Malphurs, J. (1998, April). *Jealousy protests in infants of intrusive and withdrawn mothers*. Paper presented at the meeting of the 11th Biennial International Conference on Infant Studies, Atlanta.

64. For each level, it depicts: Jones, N., Hart, S., & Field, T. (2000, July). Infant jealousy and attachment patterns in infants of depressed mothers. In R. Draghi-Lorenz, Chair, *Jealousy in young infants: A new area of research*. Symposium conducted at the meeting of the 12th Biennial International Conference on Infant Studies, Brighton, UK.

67. As if unconsciously aware of being: Greenspan, S. (1992). *Infancy and early childhood.* Madison, CT: International Universities Press.

69. True playfulness consists of an infant's: Ruff, H., & Rothbart, M. (1996). *Attention and early development.* New York: Oxford University Press.

76. The task of mending the relationship: Hart, S., Field, T., del Valle, C., & Pelaez-Nogueras, M. (1998). Depressed mothers' interactions with their one-year-old infants. *Infant Behavior and Development, 21,* 519–525.

76. The task of mending the relationship: Hart, S., Jones, N., Field, T., & Lundy, B. (1999). One-year-old infants of intrusive and withdrawn depressed mothers. *Child Psychiatry and Human Development, 30,* 111–120.

77. Further, research on hot firstborns' reactions: Dunn, J., Kendrick, C., & MacNamee, R. (1981). The reaction of first-born children to the birth of a sibling: Mothers' reports. *Journal of Child Psychology and Psychiatry, 22,* 1–18.

78. However, it is rare for a very shy infant: Kagan, J. (1997). Temperament and the reactions to unfamiliarity. *Child Development, 68,* 139–143.

Chapter Six

81. This passage was written by: Brazelton, T. B. (1983). *Infants and mothers.* New York: Dell, p. 255.

Chapter Seven

97. My boys are what were once called Irish Twins: Kelsh, N., & Quindlen, A. (1998). *Siblings.* New York: Penguin, p. 99.

100. Traditionally, child development researchers: Ainsworth, M. D. S., Blehar, M., Waters, E., & Wall, E. (1978). *Patterns of attachment.* Hillsdale, NJ: Erlbaum.

101. For psychologists who study early child development: Lamb, M., Thompson, R. A., Gardner, W., & Charnov, E. (1985). *Infant-mother attachment: The origins and developmental significance of individual differences in Strange Situation behavior.* Hillsdale, NJ: Erlbaum.

101. Last, but not least, secured toddlers: Teti, D., & Ablard, K. (1989). Security of attachment and infant-sibling relationships: A laboratory study. *Child Development, 60,* 715–727.

103. Destabilized attachment status happens: Thompson, R., Lamb, M., & Estes, D. (1982). Stability of infant-mother attachment and its relationship to changing life circumstances in an unselected middle class sample. *Child Development, 53,* 144–148.

103. Margot Touris and her colleagues: Touris, M., Kromelow, S., & Harding, C. (1995). Mother-firstborn attachment and the birth of a sibling. *American Journal of Orthopsychiatry, 65,* 293–297.

103. As a number of classic studies showed: Nadelman, L., & Begun, A. (1982). The effect of the newborn on the older sibling: Mothers' questionnaires.

In M. Lamb & B. Sutton-Smith (Eds.), *Sibling relationships: Their nature and significance across the lifespan.* Hillsdale NJ: Erlbaum.

103. As a number of classic studies showed: Freud, A. (1965). *Normality and pathology in childhood.* New York: International Universities Press.

103. As a number of classic studies showed: Kendrick, C., & Dunn, J. (1982). Protest or pleasure? The response of first-born children to interactions between their mothers and infant siblings. *Journal of Child Psychology and Psychiatry,* 23, 117–129.

103. As a number of classic studies showed: Dunn, J., & Kendrick, C. (1982). *Siblings: Love, envy, and understanding.* Cambridge, MA: Harvard University Press.

104. To the contrary, there is ample: Rutter, M., & Redshaw, J. (1991). Annotation: Growing up as a twin: Twin-singleton differences in psychological development. *Journal of Child Psychology and Psychiatry,* 32, 885–895.

104. To the contrary, there is ample: Lytton, H., Singh, J., & Gallagher, L. (1995). Parenting twins. In M. Bornstein (Ed.), *Handbook of parenting* Mahwah, NJ: Erlbaum.

106. Research by Susan Harter: Harter, S., & Buddin, B. (1987). Children's understanding of the simultaneity of two emotions: A five-stage developmental acquisition sequence. *Developmental Psychology, 23,* 388–399.

106. To illustrate just how complicated: Harris, P. (1989). *Children and emotion.* Malden, MA: Blackwell, p. 106.

107. Also too young: Donaldson, S., & Westerman, M. (1986). Development of children's understanding of ambivalence and causal theories of emotions. *Developmental Psychology, 22,* 655–662.

107. As Michael Lewis of the Robert Wood Johnson: Lewis, M. (1989). Cultural differences in children's knowledge of emotional scripts. In C. Saarni & P. Harris (Eds.), *Children's understanding of emotion.* New York: Cambridge University Press.

108. One classic study reported: Legg, C., Sherick, I., & Wadland, W. (1974). Reaction of preschool children to the birth of a sibling. *Child Psychiatry and Human Development, 5,* 3–39.

110. As we know by now, jealousy: Hart, S., Field, T., del Valle, C., & Letourneau, M. (1998). Infants protest their mothers attending to an infant-size doll. *Social Development, 7,* 54–61.

113. According to Willard Hartup: Hartup, W., Laursen, B., Stewart, M., & Eastenson, A. (1988). Conflict and the friendship relations of young children. *Child Development, 59,* 1590–1600.

113. According to Willard Hartup: Hartup, W. The company they keep: Friendships and their developmental significance. *Child Development, 67,* 1–13.

114. And again, the success of the relationship: Stoneman, Z., & Brody, G. (1993). Sibling temperaments, conflict, warmth, and role asymmetry. *Child Development, 64,* 1786–1800.

114. Positive relationships with siblings: Garcia, M., Shaw, D., Winslow, E., & Yaggi, K. (2000). Destructive sibling conflict and the development of conduct problems in young boys. *Developmental Psychology, 36,* 44–53.

115. Some research showed links between: Zajonc, R. (1976). Family configuration and intelligence. *Science, 192,* 227–236.

115. As a growing body of literature: Shantz, C., & Hobart, C. (1989). Social conflict and development: Peers and siblings. In T. Berndt & G. Ladd (Eds.), *Peer relationships in child development.* New York: Wiley.

115. As a growing body of literature: Katz, L., Kramer, L., & Gottman, J. (1992). Conflict and emotions in marital, sibling, and peer relationships. In C. Shantz & W. Hartup (Eds.), *Conflict in child and adolescent development.* New York: Cambridge University Press.

115. As a growing body of literature: Stoneman, Z., & Brody, G. (1993). Sibling temperaments, conflict, warmth, and role asymmetry. *Child Development, 64,* 1786–1800.

119. The deprecating term also implies: Kluger, B. (2000, January 31). Breaking through the estrogen ceiling. *Newsweek,* p. 11.

121. Ultimately, the best way to ensure: Cummings, E. M., & O'Reilly, A. W. (1997). Fathers in family context: Effects of marital quality on child adjustment. In M. Lamb (Ed.), *The role of the father in child development* (3rd ed.). New York: Wiley.

121. These days, nuclear families: See website www.census.gov. Also see Dortch, S. (1995). Demographic forecasts: The future of kinship. American Demographics, 17, 4–6.

Chapter Eight

125. Unfortunately, as Lynne Murray: Murray, L., & Cooper, P. J. (1997). *Postpartum depression and child development.* New York: Guilford.

127. When parents talk softly: DeCasper, A. J., & Fifer, W. (1980). Of human bonding: Newborns prefer their mothers' voices. *Science, 208,* 1174–1176.

127. If you smile at a newborn infant: Brazelton, T. B., & Nugent, J. K. (1995). Neonatal Behavioral Assessment Scale. Clinics in Developmental Medicine, No. 50. Philadelphia: Lippincott.

127. If you smile at a newborn infant: Field, T., Woodson, R., Greenberg, R., & Cohen, D. (1982). Discrimination and imitation of facial expressions by neonates. *Science, 218,* 179–181.

127. Because these smiles are usually reserved: Gewirtz, J. L. (1965). The course of infant smiling in four childrearing environments in Israel. In B. Foss (Ed.), *Determinants of infant behavior* (Vol. 3). New York: Wiley.

127. Because these smiles are usually reserved: Fogel, A. (1997). *Infancy.* Minneapolis/St. Paul: West.

129. Tronick and his colleagues: Tronick, E. Z., Als, H., Adamson, L., Wise, S., & Brazelton, T. B. (1978). The infant's response to entrapment between con-

tradictory messages in face-to-face interaction. *Journal of the American Academy of Child Psychiatry, 17,* 1–13.

129. As Tiffany Field discovered: Field, T. (1984). Early interactions between infants and their postpartum depressed mothers. *Infant Behavior and Development, 7,* 527–532.

129. By one year, infants show separation distress: Ainsworth, M. D. S., Blehar, M., Waters, E., & Wall, E. (1978). *Patterns of attachment.* Hillsdale, NJ: Erlbaum.

129. By their first birthday: Hart, S., Field, T., del Valle, C., & Letourneau, M. (1998). Infants protest their mothers attending to an infant-size doll. *Social Development, 7,* 54–61.

130. By merely being shown that their infants: Hart, S., Field, T., & Neiring, G. (1998). Depressed mothers' neonates improve following the MABI and a Brazelton demonstration. *Journal of Pediatric Psychology, 23,* 351–356.

130. By merely being shown that their infants: Das Eiden, R., & Reifman, A. (1996). Effects of Brazelton demonstrations on later parenting: A meta-analysis. *Journal of Pediatric Psychology, 21,* 857–868.

139. Whether we are concerned with physical or emotional challenges: Stern, M., & Hildebrandt, K. (1986). Prematurity stereotype: Effects on mother-infant interaction. *Child Development, 57,* 308–315.

139. Whether we are concerned with physical or emotional challenges: Field, T., Estroff, D., Yando, R., del Valle, C., Malphurs, J., & Hart, S. (1996). "Depressed" mothers' perceptions of vulnerability are related to later development. *Child Psychiatry and Human Development, 27,* 43–53.

139. Whether we are concerned with physical or emotional challenges: Hart, S., Field, T., & Roitfarb, M. (1999). Depressed mothers' assessments of their neonates' behaviors. *Infant Mental Health Journal, 20,* 200–210.

141. In research where young siblings' jealousy: Roth, W. E., Gewirtz, J. L., & Markham, M. R. (2000). Maternal attention occasions and reinforces jealous behavior in twin infant pairs. *Psychological Record,* in press.

Chapter Nine

155. Any change in the expected magnitude: Hart, S., & Boroda, A. (2000, July). *Mothers' positive vocalizations exacerbate infant jealousy.* Paper presented at the American Psychological Society, Miami.

156. Dominance fights are marked by intense competition: Rochat, P. (Ed.). (1995) *The self in infancy: Theory and research.* New York: Elsevier.

156. Dominance fights are marked by intense competition: Shantz, C., & Hobart, C. (1989). Social conflict and development: Peers and siblings. In T. Berndt & G. Ladd (Eds.), *Peer relationships in child development.* New York: Wiley.

158. Certainly, as the historian Peter Stearns: Stearns, P. (1989). *Jealousy: The evolution of an emotion in American history.* New York: New York University Press.

167. This pattern results in what is perhaps the: Gewirtz, J., & Pelaez-Nogueras, M. (1992). B. F. Skinner's legacy to human infant behavior and development. *American Psychologist, 47,* 1411–1422.

168. Insight into a relationship requires more than: Kramer, L., & Baron, L. (1995). Parental perceptions of children's sibling relationships. *Family Relations, 44,* 95–103.

Chapter Ten

171. John Travolta and Jett: (1994, October 14). "Sixteen years after *Fever,* John Travolta is hot once more." *Miami Herald.*

185. Irish Twins: Kelsh, N., & Quindlen, A. (1998). Siblings. New York: Penguin, pp. 99–110.

Suggested Reading

American Academy of Pediatrics Guide to Your Child's Nutrition: Feeding Children of All Ages, William Dietz and Loraine Stern, editors, Villard Books, New York, 1999.

Baby Signs: How to Talk With Your Baby Before Your Baby Can Talk, Linda Acredolo and Susan Goodwyn, Contemporary Books, Chicago, 1996.

The Emotional Life of the Toddler, Alicia F. Lieberman, Free Press, New York, 1993.

Emotionally Intelligent Parenting: How to Raise a Self-Disciplined Responsible, Socially Skilled Child, Maurice J. Elias, Stephen E. Tobias, and Brian S. Friedlander, Three Rivers Press, New York, 1999.

Fatherneed: Why Father Care Is as Essential as Mother Care for Your Child, Kyle Pruett, Free Press, New York, 2000.

From One Child to Two: What to Expect, How to Cope, and How to Enjoy Your Growing Family, Judy Dunn, Fawcett Columbine, New York, 1995.

Games to Play with Babies, Jackie Silberg, Gryphon House, Mt. Rainier, MD, 1993.

How Babies Talk: The Magic and Mystery of Language in the First Three Years of Life, Roberta M. Golinkoff and Kathy Hirsh-Pasek, Dutton, New York, 1999.

Normal Children Have Problems Too: How Parents Can Understand and Help, Stanley Turecki with Sarah Wernick, Bantam Books, New York, 1995.

The Optimistic Child, Martin E. P. Seligman, Houghton Mifflin, Boston, 1995.

The Scientist in the Crib: Minds, Brains, and How Children Learn, Alison Gopnik, Andrew N. Meltzoff, and Patricia K. Kuhl, William Morrow, New York, 1999.

Touchpoints: Your Child's Emotional and Behavioral Development, T. Berry Brazelton, Addison-Wesley, Reading, MA, 1992.

Why Can't You Catch Me Being Good? 26 Principles of Raising Self-Confident, Well-Behaved Children, Edythe Denkin, Adams Media, Holbrook, MA, 2000.

Index

Index

Index